SMART MONEY MOVES

A Practical Guide to Personal Finance and Investing

Russell N Hatcher

MindMosaic Publishing

CONTENTS

INTRODUCTION

Welcome to a journey where financial literacy becomes your compass in the ever-shifting landscape of today's economy. "Understanding Personal Finance" isn't merely a chapter; it's the beginning of your odyssey towards financial sovereignty. In these pages lies not just a guide but a treasure map to the rich world of finance, designed to arm you with the wisdom and tools required to steer through life's fiscal waves with aplomb.

Imagine transforming every dollar into a faithful soldier marching towards your goals. As we voyage together into the realms of budgeting, saving, and astute investing, you're not merely handling money; you are architecting your destiny. Here, budgeting transcends mere planning; it becomes an art form that harmonizes your aspirations with your wallet, ensuring every penny spent is a step towards your dreams.

As our odyssey unfolds, we'll decode the enigmas of borrowing and debt, turning daunting challenges into stepping-stones towards financial liberation. Imagine dismantling the barriers of loans and repayments, transforming them into allies on your path to economic freedom.

And there's more. Delve into the intricacies of taxes and retirement planning with us, turning what once seemed like fiscal foes into pillars of your financial fortress. Mastering these elements isn't about adding digits to your bank account; it's about rewriting your narrative to one of abundance, security, and unbridled possibilities.

So, embark on this quest with eyes wide open to the potential that lies within you. This isn't about managing money. It's about unlocking a future where financial empowerment and fulfillment are not just dreams, but your new reality.

UNDERSTANDING PERSONAL FINANCE

Setting The Stage: The Importance Of Financial Literacy

In today's ever-changing economic landscape, mastering personal finance isn't just a choice—it's essential. This chapter is your guide to the financial world, giving you the tools and knowledge you need to navigate with confidence. By understanding the core principles of personal finance, you're not just handling money; you're taking control of your financial future and moving closer to your goals.

As we embark on this journey together, we'll delve into the power of budgeting, saving, and wise investing. It's about crafting a budget that aligns with your priorities, keeping track of every dollar you earn and spend, and preparing for both emergencies and future aspirations. Through strategic investments, you're not just growing wealth; you're building a strong financial foundation that can withstand any challenge.

But our journey doesn't end there. Mastering personal finance also means confidently managing borrowing and debt. From understanding loan terms to devising effective repayment strategies, you're taking proactive steps towards financial freedom, reducing stress, and improving your overall financial well-being.

Furthermore, a comprehensive grasp of personal finance includes understanding taxes and planning for retirement. By mastering tax laws and using smart tax-saving strategies, you're minimizing tax burdens and maximizing your savings potential. Early retirement planning ensures a future filled with financial security and the freedom to enjoy life's pleasures without financial worry.

Remember, mastering personal finance isn't just about numbers—it's about taking control of your financial story. By embracing these fundamental principles, you're not just managing money; you're creating a future filled with abundance, security, and endless opportunities. So, embark on this journey with confidence, knowing that you have the power to unlock a future of financial empowerment and fulfillment.

Budgeting Basics: Creating a Financial Roadmap

Let's talk about the first step towards financial success—you guessed it, creating a budget! This section is all about diving into the core principles of budgeting, giving you priceless insights and practical tools to take charge of your finances like a pro. When you embark on this journey, you're gaining the power to track your income and expenses with precision, prioritize your financial goals, and make smart decisions about your spending habits.

Think of a budget as your financial GPS—it's your roadmap to reaching financial stability and achieving your dreams. With careful planning and consistent effort, you can use your budget to not only manage your income but also control your expenses in a way that moves you closer to your big financial goals.

Now, let's bring it to life with a real-life example of a budget for an average individual or household:

Table 1: Budget Elements (continued on next page)

Income

- Pay stubs
- Bank statements
- Any other documentation of income, including salaries, wages, bonuses
- Other
- Freelance work
- Side hustles

Table 2:Budgeting Elements(continued from previous page)

Expences

- Housing:
- Rent or Mortgage: The monthly payment for rent or mortgage, including principal, interest, property taxes, and homeowners insurance.
- Utilities: Costs for electricity, gas, water, sewer, and trash removal.
- Transportation:
- Car Payment
- Gas: Estimated monthly
- Insurance
- Maintenance
- Food and Household Items: Budget for groceries, toiletries, and other household essentials.
- Healthcare:
- Health Insurance:
- Medical Expenses: Budget for copayments, prescriptions, and other medical costs not covered by insurance.
- Debt Repayment:
- Student Loans
- Credit Cards
- Entertainment:
- Dining Out
- Entertainment: Spending on movies, concerts, streaming services, and other recreational activities.
- Savings and Investments:
- Emergency Fund
- Retirement Savings:
- Other Investments: Contributions towards brokerage accounts or other investment vehicles.
- Miscellaneous Expenses:
- Clothing
- Gifts and Donations:
- Subscriptions: Costs for magazine subscriptions, subscription boxes, or other recurring expenses.
- Pet Expenses: Budget for pet food, grooming, and veterinary care if applicable.

Financial Goals

- Short-term Goals: Saving for upcoming expenses like vacations or home renovations.
- Long-term Goals: Saving for major milestones such as buying a home, funding children's education, or achieving financial independence.

Creating (and sticking to) a budget is the cornerstone of your financial journey. This means jotting down every dollar you earn and spend, then sorting them into specific categories like housing, transportation, groceries, healthcare, and more. By doing this, you'll get a bird's-eye view of your finances—where your money is coming from, and where it's going. This breakdown gives you clarity, highlighting areas where you might be overspending and opportunities to boost your savings.

But it is not just about crunching numbers; it's about understanding your spending habits. By categorizing your expenses, you might notice trends, like overspending on dining out or entertainment. That is your cue to adjust your budget and distribute those funds towards meaningful goals—like building an emergency fund or paying off debt faster.

Your budget is not just a piece of paper—it's your roadmap to financial success. It helps you prioritize your spending, make informed decisions, and work towards specific goals. And don't forget about digital budgeting tools and apps, like Microsoft Excel®, QuickBooks®, or RocketMoney®. These tools make it easy to track your expenses, customize your budget, and visualize your spending patterns—all at your fingertips.

By setting up a solid budgeting framework, you'll be able to allocate your resources strategically. Every dollar will have a purpose, whether it's going towards your emergency fund, paying off debt, or investing in your future. It's all about making intentional choices that propel you towards financial success.

Managing Debt Effectively: Strategies for Debt Repayment

Dealing with debt is a key part of your financial journey, and I'm here to be your trusted guide every step of the way. Let's jump right into this crucial topic together, shall we? We're going to delve into the several types of debt you might encounter, such as credit card debt, student loans, and mortgages, so you can grasp the unique characteristics of each one. Understanding the differences between them is essential for developing a solid plan to tackle your debt effectively.

First up, let's talk about credit card debt. This type of debt is known as revolving debt, and it refers to a type of debt that does not have a fixed number of payments, and the balance can be carried over from one month to the next, with interest being charged on the outstanding balance. The most common example of revolving debt is credit card debt. With credit cards, you have a credit limit, and you can make purchases up to that limit. You must make at least a minimum payment each month, but you can choose to pay more or less than the full balance. If you don't pay off the full balance, the remaining amount carries over to the next month, and interest is charged on it. This cycle continues until the balance is paid off or until the credit limit is reached.

Other examples of revolving debt include lines of credit and home equity lines of credit (HELOCs). Revolving debt offers flexibility in terms of payments but can also lead to high-interest charges if balances are not paid off promptly. Credit card debt often comes with high interest rates, making it particularly challenging to pay off. It's usually accumulated from everyday expenses or unexpected emergencies, and if left unchecked, it can quickly spiral out of control. That's why it's crucial to have strategies in place to manage and reduce your credit card debt.

Next on our list is student loan debt. This is installment debt taken on to finance higher education, and it can vary widely in terms of interest rates and repayment options. Student loans often come with more favorable terms compared to other types of debt, but they can still be a significant financial burden, especially for recent graduates. Understanding the ins and outs of student loan repayment plans and forgiveness programs can help you navigate this aspect of your financial journey more effectively.

For installment debt, such as student loans, several repayment options may be available, depending on the terms of the loan and the lender. Some common repayment options include:

- Standard Repayment Plan: This is the default repayment plan offered by most lenders. It involves making fixed monthly payments over a set period, typically 10 years. The monthly payments are calculated to ensure that the loan is fully repaid by the end of the term.

- Graduated Repayment Plan: With this plan, payments start out lower and gradually increase over time, usually every two years. This can be beneficial for borrowers who expect their income to increase steadily over time.
- Income-Driven Repayment Plans: These plans adjust your monthly payments based on your income and family size. There are several types of income-driven repayment plans, including Income-Based Repayment (IBR), Pay As You Earn (PAYE), Revised Pay As You Earn (REPAYE), and Income-Contingent Repayment (ICR). These plans typically cap your monthly payments at a percentage of your discretionary income and extend the repayment term to 20 or 25 years, after which any remaining balance may be forgiven.
- Extended Repayment Plan: This plan allows you to extend the repayment term beyond the standard 10 years, resulting in lower monthly payments. However, this also means paying more interest over the life of the loan.
- Consolidation: Borrowers with multiple federal student loans can consolidate them into a single loan with a single monthly payment. This can simplify repayment and may also offer access to certain repayment plans, such as income-driven repayment.

It's important for borrowers to research and understand their repayment options carefully to choose the plan that best fits their financial situation and goals. Additionally, private student loans may offer different repayment options compared to federal loans, so borrowers should consult with their lender for specific details.

Lastly, let's discuss mortgages. A mortgage is another type of installment loan taken out to buy a home, and it's typically considered "good debt" because it's an investment in an appreciating asset. Mortgages generally come with lower interest rates compared to credit card debt, making them more manageable over the long term. However, it's still important to stay on top of your mortgage payments to avoid foreclosure and protect your home.

But wait! What about car loans? While both mortgages and auto loans are types of installment loans, there are several key differences between them:

- Purpose: Mortgages are loans used to buy real estate, typically homes or property. Auto loans, on the other hand, are loans used to finance the purchase of a vehicle, such as a car, truck, or motorcycle.
- Collateral: Mortgages are secured loans, meaning the property being bought serves as collateral for the loan. If the borrower does not repay the mortgage, the lender has the right to foreclose on the property and sell it to recoup their losses. Auto loans are also secured loans, with the vehicle serving as collateral. If the borrower defaults on the loan, the lender can repossess the vehicle to satisfy the debt.
- Loan Amounts: Mortgages tend to involve larger loan amounts than auto loans, reflecting the higher cost of real estate. Auto loans typically have smaller loan amounts, based on the value of the vehicle being bought.
- Loan Terms: Mortgages typically have longer loan terms compared to auto loans. It's common for mortgages to have loan terms of 15, 20, or 30 years, while auto loans typically have terms ranging from 3 to 7 years.

- <u>Interest Rates</u>: Interest rates for mortgages and auto loans can vary based on factors such as creditworthiness, market conditions, and loan terms. However, mortgage interest rates tend to be lower than auto loan interest rates, reflecting the lower risk to lenders due to the collateral involved.
- <u>Tax Deductibility</u>: In some cases, the interest paid on a mortgage may be tax-deductible, providing potential tax benefits for homeowners. Interest on auto loans, however, is generally not tax-deductible.

Now that we've got a good grasp of these distinct types of debt, let's dive into the exciting part—putting practical strategies into action to lighten your debt load. Let me share some actionable tips to empower you on your journey to financial freedom.

First, create a budget and stick to it religiously. Track your income and expenses, find areas where you can cut back on spending, and give any extra funds towards debt repayment. This disciplined approach can help you stay on track with your financial goals and accelerate your journey towards debt freedom no matter which strategy you choose.

Tip #1

The Avalanche Method One effective strategy is prioritizing your debt payments, also known as the avalanche method. Start by making a list of all your debts (remember that budget we made earlier?), including the outstanding balance, interest rate, and minimum monthly payment. Then, focus on paying off high-interest debts first, such as credit card debt. By giving extra funds towards these debts while making minimum payments on others, you can save money on interest and pay off your debts more quickly.

Tip #2

The Snowball Method   On the other hand, the snowball method of repaying debt is a debt reduction strategy where you prioritize paying off debts from smallest to largest balance, regardless of interest rate. Here's how it works:

- List Your Debts: Start by making a list of all your debts, including the outstanding balance, minimum monthly payment, and interest rate.
- Order by Balance: Arrange your debts in order from smallest to largest balance, regardless of interest rate. This means the debt with the smallest balance will be at the top of your list.
- Pay Minimums: Continue making the minimum monthly payments on all your debts except for the one with the smallest balance.
- Pay Extra: Allocate any extra funds you have towards paying off the debt with the smallest balance. This could include using extra income, cutting expenses, or selling items to generate additional cash.
- Snowball Effect: Once you've paid off the smallest debt, take the amount you were paying towards it (including the minimum payment) and apply it to the next debt on your list. This creates a "snowball" effect, where the amount you're putting towards debt repayment grows larger with each debt you pay off.
- Repeat: Keep repeating this process, tackling each debt in succession from smallest to largest, until you're debt-free.

The snowball method is effective because it provides quick wins by paying off smaller debts first, which can help motivate you to stick with your debt repayment plan. While it may not save you as much in interest compared to other strategies that prioritize high-interest debts, the psychological boost of seeing debts disappear can be invaluable for many people.

Tip #3

Consolidation Another helpful tip is to explore debt consolidation options. Merging your debts into a single loan with a lower interest rate can make repayment more manageable and streamlined. For example, you might consider transferring high-interest credit card balances to a new credit card with a lower promotional interest rate or taking out a personal loan to join multiple debts into one monthly payment.

When considering a consolidation loan, there are several factors that you should be cautious about:

- Interest Rates: While consolidation loans often offer lower interest rates compared to credit cards or other high-interest debts, it's essential to carefully review the terms of the consolidation loan to ensure that the interest rate is indeed lower. Some consolidation loans may come with introductory rates that increase after a certain period, potentially leaving you with higher interest costs in the long run.
- Fees and Charges: Be aware of any fees or charges associated with the consolidation loan, such as origination fees, application fees, or prepayment penalties. These fees can add to the overall cost of the loan and diminish the potential savings from combining your debts.
- Loan Terms: Pay attention to the repayment terms of the consolidation loan, including the length of the repayment period and the monthly payment amount. While longer loan terms may result in lower monthly payments, they also mean paying more in interest over the life of the loan.

- Impact on Credit Score: Combining your debts with a consolidation loan can have both positive and negative effects on your credit score. Closing multiple accounts or opening a new loan can affect your credit utilization ratio and the average age of your accounts, which are factors that influence your credit score. Additionally, applying for a consolidation loan may result in a hard inquiry on your credit report, which can temporarily lower your score.
- Continued Spending Habits: Merging your debts can provide temporary relief by simplifying your monthly payments and potentially reducing your interest costs. However, it's crucial to address the underlying issues that led to the accumulation of debt in the first place. Without addressing spending habits and implementing a budget and financial plan, there's a risk of falling back into debt even after consolidating.

Overall, while consolidation loans can be a useful tool for managing and reducing debt, it's essential to approach them with caution and carefully consider the potential benefits and drawbacks. It's also advisable to consult with a financial advisor or credit counselor to assess your options and figure out the best course of action for your individual financial situation.

Tip #4

Negotiation   Next, let's explore the power of negotiation. Whether it's negotiating lower interest rates with creditors or setting up more manageable payment plans, there are often opportunities to work with lenders to make your debt more manageable. Here's how you can approach it:

Let's imagine Bill, a hardworking individual who's found himself struggling to keep up with his credit card payments due to unexpected medical expenses. Here's how Bill could negotiate with his creditors to reduce his debt:

- Preparation: Bill gathers all his credit card statements and takes note of his outstanding balances, interest rates, and minimum monthly payments. He also reviews his budget to decide how much he can realistically afford to pay towards his debts each month.
- Initiating Contact: Bill reaches out to his credit card companies as soon as he realizes he's unable to make his payments on time. He explains his situation honestly, emphasizing the unexpected medical expenses that have strained his finances.
- Proposal: Bill proposes a reduced payment plan to his creditors, explaining that he can't afford to make the full minimum payments each month. He suggests a lower monthly payment that he can manage while still covering his essential expenses.
- Exploring Options: Bill also asks if there's any possibility of lowering the interest rates on his credit cards to make his payments more manageable. He mentions that he's been a loyal customer for many years and would appreciate any help the creditors can offer.
- Negotiation: Bill stays calm and respectful during the negotiation process, even if the creditors initially push back on his proposals. He listens to their concerns and offers to provide documentation of his financial situation if needed.
- Documenting Agreements: If Bill and his creditors reach an agreement, he makes sure to get the details in writing and keeps records of all communication. This includes the new payment plan, any changes to interest rates, and any other

terms agreed upon.

By proactively negotiating with his creditors and advocating for himself, Bill can find a solution that helps him manage his debt and alleviate financial stress. He can now focus on rebuilding his finances and moving forward with confidence.

Remember, creditors are often willing to negotiate, especially if it means they're more likely to recover at least some of the money owed to them. Don't be afraid to advocate for yourself and explore all available options for reducing your debt burden.

Don't hesitate to seek help if you're struggling with debt. Reach out to your creditors to discuss repayment options, such as hardship programs or modified payment plans. You can also consider working with a reputable credit counseling agency for personalized advice and support.

With these powerful strategies in your toolkit, you'll be armed and ready to take control of your debt and make real progress towards achieving financial freedom. It's time to take charge of your financial future and build a brighter tomorrow for yourself and your loved ones.

So, if you're ready to tackle your debt head-on and regain control of your financial future, let's get started. Together, we'll pave the way for a brighter tomorrow, one step at a time.

Building an Emergency Fund: The Foundation of Financial Stability

Having an emergency fund is like having a financial safety net—it's a crucial part of any solid financial plan. In this section, we'll delve into why having an emergency fund is so important and provide practical guidance on how to build and maintain one.

Having an emergency fund is incredibly important for several reasons. Firstly, it provides a sense of financial security by acting as a safety net for unexpected expenses like medical emergencies or car repairs. Without it, people may resort to using credit cards or loans, potentially leading to debt and financial strain. Secondly, having an emergency fund brings peace of mind. Instead of worrying about how to cover unexpected expenses, individuals can focus on finding solutions calmly. This can significantly reduce stress and anxiety related to financial emergencies.

Furthermore, an emergency fund helps individuals avoid debt. By having cash on hand to cover expenses upfront, they can avoid accumulating high-interest debt that can be challenging to repay. Maintaining financial stability is another key benefit of having an emergency fund. Financial emergencies can disrupt long-term financial goals, but with a safety net in place, individuals can stay on track and continue working towards their savings and investment objectives. Lastly, an emergency fund provides flexibility and freedom. It allows individuals to handle unexpected events without relying on outside assistance, giving them the autonomy to address situations on their own terms.

So how do you start setting up an emergency fund, you may ask. First and foremost, we'll determine the appropriate size of your emergency fund. To help us out, we'll look at how one woman met the challenge head on.

Meet Emily, a vibrant and ambitious young woman with a zest for life. Emily has always been financially responsible, but lately, she's been feeling the weight of uncertainty looming over her. She's heard about the importance of having an emergency fund, but she's not quite sure where to start.

One sunny afternoon, Emily decides to take matters into her own hands. Armed with determination and a notebook, she sets out to tackle the daunting task of building her emergency fund.

First, Emily considers how to determine the appropriate size of her emergency fund. She knows that everyone's financial situation is different, so she takes stock of her monthly expenses, including rent, utilities, groceries, and other essentials (here's our budget again!). After some careful calculation, Emily decides that having three to six months' worth of expenses saved up would provide her with a solid financial cushion in case of emergencies.

While there isn't a one-size-fits-all formula for determining the size of an emergency fund, a commonly recommended guideline is to aim for three to six months' worth of living expenses. However, this guideline may vary depending on individual circumstances such as income stability, job security, family size, and financial obligations.

To calculate the size of your emergency fund, start by tallying up your essential monthly expenses, including rent or mortgage payments, utilities, groceries, transportation, insurance premiums, debt payments, and other necessities. Once you have a total monthly expense amount, multiply it by the number of months you want to cover with your emergency fund (e.g., three months, six months).

It's important to consider factors such as the stability of your income, the likelihood of facing unexpected expenses, and any potential sources of financial support (such as a spouse's income or other forms of assistance) when determining the appropriate size of your emergency fund. Additionally, if you have specific financial goals or concerns (such as saving for a major purchase or dealing with medical expenses), you may want to adjust the size of your emergency fund accordingly. Ultimately, the size of your emergency fund should provide you with a sense of financial security and peace of mind, knowing that you have a financial cushion to fall back on in case of unexpected events or emergencies. Adjustments to the size of your emergency fund may be necessary over time as your financial situation evolves.

Next, Emily devises a plan to save money effectively to contribute to her emergency fund. She decides to start small by setting aside a portion of her paycheck each month. She looks for ways to cut back on non-essential expenses, like dining out and shopping, and redirects those funds towards her emergency fund. Emily also considers setting up automatic transfers from her checking account to her savings account to ensure consistent contributions.

Ensuring consistent contributions to an emergency fund is crucial for several reasons:

- Building Habit: Consistency builds habit. By making regular contributions to your emergency fund, you establish a routine of saving that becomes ingrained in your financial behavior. This habit makes it easier to prioritize saving and ensures that you're continually working towards your financial goals.
- Steady Growth: Consistent contributions lead to steady growth of your emergency fund over time. Even if you can only contribute a small amount each month, those contributions add up over time, helping you build a substantial financial cushion to weather unexpected expenses or emergencies.
- Emergency Preparedness: Life is unpredictable, and emergencies can happen at any time. By consistently contributing to your emergency fund, you ensure that it's always ready to provide financial support when you need it most. This preparedness gives you peace of mind knowing that you have a safety net in place to handle unforeseen circumstances.
- Avoiding Procrastination: Consistent contributions help you avoid the trap of procrastination. It's easy to put off saving for emergencies, especially when other financial priorities compete for your attention. However, consistent contributions ensure that you're making progress towards your savings goals and

avoid falling behind.

- Maintaining Discipline: Regular contributions to your emergency fund require discipline and commitment. By staying disciplined in your saving habits, you reinforce positive financial behavior and cultivate a mindset of responsibility and preparedness.

As Emily continues to make progress towards her savings goal, she recognizes the importance of insurance in her financial protection. She reviews her existing insurance policies, including health insurance, renters insurance, and car insurance, to ensure that she's adequately covered in case of emergencies. She also considers additional insurance options, such as disability insurance and life insurance, to provide further peace of mind.

Through her journey to build her emergency fund, Emily learns valuable lessons about financial responsibility and resilience. With each contribution to her fund, she feels a sense of empowerment and security knowing that she's taking proactive steps to safeguard her financial future. And as she looks ahead, Emily knows that she's well-equipped to handle whatever life throws her way, thanks to her diligent savings habits and comprehensive insurance coverage.

By setting up and growing an emergency fund, you'll be taking proactive steps to safeguard yourself against unexpected expenses and financial hardships. With the knowledge and tools provided in this section, you'll be well-equipped to weather any storm that comes your way and achieve greater peace of mind knowing that you have a financial safety net to fall back on.

Chapter Summary

Chapter 1 of "Smart Money Moves" serves as a comprehensive guide to mastering your financial journey. It began by emphasizing the indispensability of personal finance in today's economic landscape, positioning it not just as a choice but as an essential skill for taking control of your financial future. It also covered key areas such as budgeting, saving, investing, managing debt, understanding taxes, and planning for retirement.

Budgeting Basics highlighted the importance of creating a budget as a roadmap to financial stability and goal achievement. The first section offered practical insights into tracking income and expenses, categorizing spending, and using digital tools to manage finances effectively.

Managing Debt Effectively was addressed next, offering strategies for tackling distinct types of debt like credit card debt, student loans, mortgages, and auto loans. This section explained the differences between these debts and provides actionable tips for debt repayment, including prioritizing payments, exploring consolidation options, and negotiating with creditors.

Building an Emergency Fund was presented as the foundation of financial stability. This section underscored the importance of having an emergency fund to handle unexpected expenses and provided guidance on deciding the appropriate size of the fund, saving money effectively, and understanding the role of insurance in financial protection.

By embracing the principles outlined in this chapter, you can embark on your financial journey with confidence, equipped with the knowledge and tools needed to navigate challenges and achieve your long-term financial goals.

INVESTING FUNDAMENTALS

Welcome to Chapter 2, where we're about to embark on an exciting journey into the world of investing. In this chapter, we'll delve deep into the fundamental principles of investing, arming you with the indispensable knowledge needed to make savvy decisions and cultivate wealth over the long haul. Whether you're a seasoned investor or just starting out, by the end of this chapter, you'll be equipped with the insights and tools to navigate the investment landscape with confidence and clarity. So, let's dive in and uncover the secrets to building a brighter financial future through smart investing.

Introduction to Investing: Key Concepts and Terminology

Let's kick things off by shedding light on the sometimes-daunting world of investing. At its core, investing involves allocating resources, usually money, with the anticipation of reaping a return or profit down the road. It's about making your money work for you, instead of allowing it to remain stagnant or idle. By investing wisely, you're taking proactive steps towards growing your wealth and achieving your financial goals. So, think of investing as a strategic tool to leverage your resources and build a brighter financial future.

One fundamental principle in investing revolves around the relationship between risk and return. The potential for higher returns typically goes hand in hand with higher levels of risk. This means that investments offering the possibility of significant gains often carry greater uncertainty and the potential for losses.

When constructing your investment portfolio, it's essential to consider your risk tolerance—the degree of uncertainty or volatility you're comfortable with regarding your investments. Understanding your risk tolerance is crucial because it helps align your investment choices with your financial objectives and emotional comfort level.

Meet Alfie, a 30-something-year-old who's ready to dip his toes into the world of investing. Alfie has always been financially savvy, but he's new to the investment game and eager to learn. As he begins his investment journey, Alfie takes a moment to assess his risk tolerance—the amount of uncertainty he's willing to stomach in pursuit of potential returns.

After careful reflection, Alfie realizes he has a high tolerance for risk. He's willing to weather the ups and downs of the market in exchange for the possibility of higher returns. With this in mind, Alfie decides to allocate a larger portion of his investment portfolio to stocks and other growth-oriented assets. He understands that while these investments may be more volatile in the short term, they have the potential to deliver significant gains over the long term.

On the other hand, Alfie's friend Sarah, who's also in her 30s but has a more cautious approach to investing, opts for a different strategy. Sarah prioritizes capital preservation and stability, preferring to minimize the risk of large fluctuations in the value of her investments. As a result, Sarah chooses to allocate a greater portion of her portfolio to bonds and other fixed-income securities, which offer more predictable returns and lower volatility.

By comprehending and acknowledging their respective risk tolerances, both Alfie and Sarah can construct investment portfolios that align with their financial goals and emotional comfort levels. Alfie sets himself up for the potential of higher returns with his growth-oriented strategy, while Sarah prioritizes stability and capital preservation with her conservative approach.

By tailoring their investment strategies to their risk tolerances, Alfie and Sarah position themselves for greater success and peace of mind in their investment journeys.

Another crucial concept in investing is compounding, which is the snowball effect of your investment gains generating additional gains over time. Here's how it works: when you earn a return on your initial investment, those earnings are reinvested along with your original capital. As a result, your investment grows not only on the initial amount but also on the accumulated earnings.

The magic of compounding lies in its exponential growth potential. The earlier you start investing, the more time your money must compound, allowing your investments to grow at an accelerating rate over time. Even modest returns can compound into significant wealth over extended periods.

For example, let's say you invest $1,000 and earn a 10% return in the first year, resulting in $100 in gains. In the second year, if you earn another 10% return, you're not just earning 10% on your initial $1,000 investment but also on the $100 in gains from the previous year. This compounding effect continues to snowball over time, amplifying the growth of your investment portfolio.

By understanding the power of compounding and starting to invest early, you can harness its potential to build substantial wealth over the long term. So, don't underestimate the impact of time on your investments—start investing as soon as possible to maximize the benefits of compounding and secure a brighter financial future.

Let's consider an alternative example. Imagine you invest $1,000 in a high-risk investment that promises double-digit returns. Unfortunately, the investment performs poorly in the first year, resulting in a loss of 10%, or $100. In the second year, you decide to stick with the same investment, hoping for a rebound. However, instead of recovering, the investment experiences another 10% loss, resulting in another $100 loss.

Now, not only have you lost $100 in the first year, but you're also losing another $100 in the second year, amplifying your losses. This negative compounding effect continues to erode the value of your investment portfolio over time, making it increasingly challenging to recover from the initial setbacks.

In this scenario, the lack of proper risk management and understanding of the potential downsides of the investment led to significant losses. It highlights the importance of carefully assessing risk and diversifying your investment portfolio to mitigate potential losses and safeguard your financial well-being over the long term.

Types of Investments: Stocks, Bonds, Mutual Funds, and ETFs

Now, let's delve into the diverse array of investment options at your disposal. Stocks, for starters, represent ownership shares in a company. They have the potential to yield significant returns, making them an attractive choice for investors seeking growth opportunities. However, it's important to note that stocks also entail higher levels of risk due to their susceptibility to market fluctuations and company-specific factors.

On the flip side, we have bonds, which are debt securities issued by governments or corporations. When you invest in bonds, you're essentially lending money to the issuer in exchange for periodic interest payments and the return of the principal amount at maturity. Bonds are valued for their relatively stable and predictable income stream, making them an appealing option for investors prioritizing capital preservation and steady income. Compared to stocks, bonds typically carry lower risk, making them a popular choice for risk-averse investors or those with shorter investment horizons.

Stocks offer the potential for growth but come with higher risk, while bonds provide stability and income with lower risk. By understanding the characteristics and risk profiles of each asset class, you can tailor your investment strategy to align with your financial goals, risk tolerance, and time horizon. Whether you opt for stocks, bonds, or a combination of both, diversifying your investment portfolio can help you achieve a balanced approach that balances potential returns with risk mitigation.

Mutual funds and exchange-traded funds (ETFs) are investment vehicles that pool money from multiple investors to invest in a diversified portfolio of assets. Mutual funds are actively managed by professional fund managers, while ETFs typically track a specific index and are passively managed.

To provide a practical example, let's imagine you have $10,000 available for investment. With this amount, you have the flexibility to diversify your portfolio across different asset classes to optimize your risk-return profile.

For instance, you might decide to allocate $5,000 of your investment capital into a diversified stock mutual fund. This fund pools investments from various investors and spreads them across a wide range of stocks, providing you with exposure to different companies and industries. This investment offers the potential for significant growth over the long term, as stock prices fluctuate based on market conditions and company performance.

Now, with the remaining $5,000, you could opt to invest in a bond ETF (Exchange-Traded Fund). A bond ETF consists of a basket of bonds valued for their fixed interest payments and return of principal at maturity, offering a more stable and predictable income stream compared to stocks. By investing in a bond ETF, you're effectively lending money to the issuer in exchange for regular interest payments and the eventual return of your investment. This allocation serves to mitigate risk within your portfolio, providing stability and income even during periods of market volatility.

By diversifying your investment across both stocks and bonds, you're able to strike a balance between growth potential and risk mitigation. While the stock mutual fund offers the possibility of higher returns over time, the bond ETF provides stability and income, helping to cushion your portfolio against market fluctuations. This balanced approach to asset allocation allows you to maximize the benefits of both asset classes while minimizing overall risk, enhancing the resilience and performance of your investment portfolio.

Risk Management: Diversification and Asset Allocation Strategies

Finally, let's turn our attention to risk management strategies, which play a crucial role in constructing a resilient investment portfolio. Diversification is a key principle that involves spreading your investments across various asset classes, industries, and geographic regions. By diversifying, you reduce the impact of any single investment's performance on your overall portfolio. You're not putting all your eggs in one basket. For example, if one sector or region experiences a downturn, other sectors or regions may continue to perform well, helping to offset potential losses.

Asset allocation is another essential aspect of risk management. It involves strategically distributing your investments among different asset classes, such as stocks, bonds, real estate, and cash equivalents, based on your investment goals, risk tolerance, and time horizon. The goal of asset allocation is to create a well-balanced portfolio that aligns with your financial objectives while managing risk effectively. For instance, if you have a long investment horizon and a high-risk tolerance, you might allocate a larger portion of your portfolio to stocks for growth potential. On the other hand, if you have a shorter time horizon or a lower risk tolerance, you may opt for a more conservative asset allocation with a higher proportion of bonds or cash equivalents to preserve capital and reduce volatility.

By incorporating diversification and asset allocation into your investment strategy, you're able to mitigate risk, enhance portfolio resilience, and improve the likelihood of achieving your financial goals over the long term. These risk management strategies provide a solid foundation for building a well-rounded investment portfolio that can weather market fluctuations and deliver sustainable returns.

Let's illustrate this with an example: imagine you're a 30-year-old investor with a long investment horizon ahead of you and a moderate risk tolerance. Given your age and risk tolerance, you recognize that you have the luxury of time to weather market volatility and pursue higher growth opportunities.

You might decide to allocate a larger portion of your investment portfolio to stocks, which historically have provided higher returns over the long term but come with greater volatility. By investing more heavily in stocks, you're aiming to capitalize on their growth potential and maximize your wealth accumulation over the decades to come.

At the same time, you're mindful of the need for stability and capital preservation, especially as you progress towards retirement. To achieve this balance, you might allocate a smaller portion of your portfolio to bonds, which offer more predictable returns and act as a buffer against stock market fluctuations. Bonds provide stability and income, helping to offset the higher risk associated with stocks.

As you near retirement age, your investment strategy may evolve to reflect your changing financial needs and risk tolerance. With fewer years until retirement, you may gradually shift towards a more conservative asset allocation by reducing your exposure to stocks and increasing your allocation to bonds and other fixed-income investments. This adjustment aims to protect your savings and minimize the impact of market downturns as you approach retirement.

In summary, as a 30-year-old investor with a moderate risk tolerance, you initially prioritize growth by allocating a larger portion of your portfolio to stocks. As you progress through different life stages and near retirement, you gradually transition to a more conservative asset allocation to safeguard your savings and ensure financial security in your golden years.

Chapter Summary

In this chapter, we embarked on a journey into the world of investing, demystifying its complexities and unveiling its potential for financial growth. Investing, at its core, involves deploying resources, typically money, with the expectation of generating a return or profit in the future. It's about proactively managing your money to achieve your financial aspirations and secure a brighter future.

We explored the fundamental principle of risk and return, understanding that higher potential returns often accompany higher levels of risk. By grasping this concept, investors can align their investment choices with their risk tolerance and financial goals.

Furthermore, we delved into the concept of compounding, witnessing its remarkable ability to multiply investment gains over time. Through examples, we saw how starting to invest early and allowing investments to compound can lead to significant wealth accumulation.

Exploring the diverse types of investments, such as stocks and bonds, we learned how each asset class offers distinct characteristics and risk profiles. By understanding these differences, investors can craft diversified portfolios that balance growth potential with risk mitigation.

Lastly, we explored risk management strategies, including diversification and asset allocation. By spreading investments across different asset classes and strategically allocating resources, investors can reduce the impact of market fluctuations and enhance portfolio resilience.

By understanding these fundamental investing concepts and strategies, you'll be well-equipped to embark on your investment journey with confidence. Remember, investing is a long-term endeavor, so stay focused on your goals and remain disciplined in your approach. Happy investing!

DEVELOPING AN INVESTMENT STRATEGY

Setting Financial Goals: Short-term vs. Long-term Objectives

Setting clear financial goals is the foundation upon which a successful investment strategy is built. When you establish specific objectives for your finances, you are creating a roadmap that guides your investment decisions and actions. These goals serve as the guiding light that helps you stay focused, motivated, and accountable in your financial journey.

Whether your aspirations are short-term or long-term, defining your financial goals is crucial for several reasons. Firstly, it provides you with a sense of purpose and direction, giving your financial decisions a clear meaning. By knowing what you are working towards, you can prioritize your efforts and resources accordingly.

For instance, if you are saving for a short-term goal like a dream vacation or a new car, having a specific target amount and timeline in mind can help you determine how much you need to save each month and what investment vehicles are most suitable for achieving that goal within the desired timeframe.

For instance, if your short-term goal involves saving for a down payment on a house within the next five years, you may prioritize capital preservation and liquidity. In this scenario, low-risk investment options such as high-yield savings accounts or bonds could be suitable choices. These investments offer stability and the flexibility to access funds when needed, ensuring that your savings are preserved and available for your upcoming financial milestone.

On the other hand, if you are planning for long-term objectives such as retirement or your children's education, setting clear financial goals allows you to break down these larger aspirations into manageable milestones. This approach not only makes the daunting task of saving for retirement more achievable but also enables you to track your progress over time and adjust as needed.

For long-term goals that may span several decades, a more aggressive approach may be warranted. In this case, you could consider a diversified portfolio comprising a mix of stocks and bonds. Stocks offer the potential for higher returns over the long term, albeit with greater volatility, while bonds provide stability and income. By diversifying your investments across different asset classes, you can balance risk and potential returns, positioning yourself for long-term financial growth and security.

Defining your financial goals is the cornerstone of a successful investment strategy because it provides you with a sense of purpose, direction, and motivation. It empowers you to take control of your financial future, make informed decisions, and work towards realizing your dreams and aspirations.

Short-term goals refer to objectives you intend to accomplish within the near future, typically within the next few years. In contrast, long-term goals encompass aspirations that extend over a decade or more. Distinguishing between these two types of goals is crucial for crafting an appropriate investment strategy.

By aligning your investment strategy with the timeline and nature of your financial goals, you can optimize your chances of achieving success and realizing your aspirations. Whether you're saving for a short-term milestone or planning for the distant future, tailoring your investment approach accordingly ensures that your financial resources are effectively deployed to support your objectives.

Assessing Risk Tolerance: Finding Your Comfort Zone

Understanding your risk tolerance is paramount when devising your investment strategy as it directly influences your financial journey's trajectory. Risk tolerance denotes your capacity to endure fluctuations in the value of your investments without succumbing to panic or making impulsive decisions.

It reflects your psychological and emotional preparedness to withstand the inherent uncertainties and volatility of the financial markets. A thorough assessment of your risk tolerance involves evaluating factors such as your financial goals, investment timeframe, and comfort level with market fluctuations.

By comprehending your risk tolerance, you can align your investment decisions with your individual preferences and circumstances. For instance, if you have a high risk tolerance, you may feel comfortable investing in assets with greater volatility and potential for higher returns, such as stocks. Conversely, if you have a low risk tolerance, you may prefer more stable and predictable investments, such as bonds or cash equivalents.

Ultimately, understanding your risk tolerance empowers you to construct an investment portfolio that not only aligns with your financial goals but also provides peace of mind during periods of market turbulence. It enables you to stay disciplined and committed to your long-term investment strategy, avoiding impulsive actions that could derail your financial objectives.

By acknowledging and embracing your risk tolerance, you can tailor your investment approach to suit your individual preferences and objectives, fostering confidence and resilience in your financial journey.

Several factors influence your risk tolerance, shaping your willingness and ability to withstand fluctuations in the value of your investments. These factors include your age, financial situation, investment knowledge, and emotional temperament.

Age is a significant determinant of risk tolerance. Younger investors with a longer time horizon ahead of them tend to have a higher risk tolerance. They have more time to recover from market downturns and capitalize on the potential for higher returns offered by growth-oriented assets like stocks. In contrast, older investors nearing retirement typically have a lower risk tolerance as they have less time to recover from losses and prioritize capital preservation to ensure a secure retirement.

Your financial situation also plays a crucial role in determining your risk tolerance. Factors such as your income, savings, and overall financial stability influence your capacity to take on risk. Individuals with ample financial resources may feel more comfortable assuming greater investment risk, knowing they have a financial cushion to fall back on in case of losses. Conversely, those with limited resources may opt for more conservative investments to safeguard their financial security.

Investment knowledge and experience are essential factors that shape your risk tolerance. Investors with a deep understanding of financial markets and investment principles may feel more confident taking on higher levels of risk, knowing they can make informed decisions and manage potential losses effectively. Conversely, novice investors or those with limited investment knowledge may prefer conservative strategies to minimize the risk of making costly mistakes.

Emotional temperament also plays a significant role in risk tolerance. Some individuals may have a natural inclination towards risk-taking and feel exhilarated by the prospect of potential gains, while others may feel anxious or stressed in volatile market conditions. Understanding your emotional response to investment fluctuations is crucial in determining your risk tolerance and devising an investment strategy that aligns with your comfort level.

In summary, your risk tolerance is influenced by a combination of factors including your age, financial situation, investment knowledge, and emotional temperament. By considering these factors and assessing your individual risk tolerance, you can construct an investment portfolio that strikes the right balance between risk and potential returns, supporting your financial goals and objectives.

Let's consider Sarah, a 30-year-old investor with a high risk tolerance, as a real-life example of risk tolerance in action. Sarah recognizes that she has several decades ahead of her before retirement and decides to capitalize on the long-term growth potential of stocks by allocating a significant portion of her investment portfolio to them.

Despite the inevitable market fluctuations and occasional downturns, Sarah remains steadfast in her investment strategy. She understands that volatility is a natural part of investing in stocks and doesn't let short-term market movements shake her confidence. Instead, she focuses on the bigger picture and remains committed to her long-term financial goals.

Sarah's high risk tolerance allows her to weather market turbulence without succumbing to panic or making impulsive decisions. She views market downturns as opportunities to buy quality stocks at discounted prices, leveraging dollar-cost averaging to accumulate shares over time.

Sarah's confidence in her investment strategy is bolstered by her thorough research and understanding of the companies she invests in. She conducts due diligence before making investment decisions, assessing factors such as the company's financial health, growth prospects, and competitive positioning.

As a result of her high risk tolerance and disciplined approach to investing, Sarah's portfolio experiences significant growth over the years. Despite the occasional setbacks, she remains focused on her long-term financial objectives, knowing that staying the course and remaining invested in quality companies will ultimately yield favorable outcomes.

In summary, Sarah's real-life example illustrates how risk tolerance influences investment decisions and behavior. Her willingness to embrace risk and stay committed to her long-term investment strategy allows her to navigate market volatility with confidence and achieve her financial goals over time.

Creating a Personalized Investment Plan: Matching Goals with Strategies

Once you've clarified your financial goals and gauged your risk tolerance, the next step is to develop a tailored investment plan that reflects your unique circumstances and aspirations. This personalized plan serves as a roadmap for achieving your objectives while navigating the inherent risks of investing.

Your investment plan should start by clearly defining your financial goals, whether they involve saving for retirement, funding education expenses, purchasing a home, or building wealth over the long term. The acronym SMART stands for Specific, Measurable, Achievable, Relevant, and Time-bound. It is a mnemonic device used to guide the setting of clear and effective goals. Let's break down each component:

Specific: Goals should be clear and specific, leaving no room for ambiguity or confusion. Instead of saying, "I want to save money," a specific goal would be, "I want to save $5,000 for a down payment on a house within the next two years."

Measurable: Goals should be quantifiable, allowing progress to be tracked and evaluated. This means defining criteria for measuring success. Using the previous example, the measurable aspect would be the $5,000 savings target.

Achievable: Goals should be realistic and attainable given the resources, time, and constraints available. Setting goals that are too far-fetched or beyond your control can lead to frustration and discouragement. It's important to set goals that challenge you but are still within reach with effort and commitment.

R elevant: Goals should be aligned with your overall objectives and values, ensuring that they are meaningful and worthwhile to pursue. Consider whether the goal contributes to your long-term aspirations and whether it is relevant to your current circumstances and priorities.

T ime-bound: Goals should have a defined timeframe or deadline for completion. This helps create a sense of urgency and accountability, motivating action and preventing procrastination. Establishing deadlines also allows for progress to be monitored and adjustments to be made as needed.

By following the SMART criteria, you can ensure that your goals are well-defined, achievable, and aligned with your vision for the future. This approach increases the likelihood of success and provides a framework for effective goal-setting and execution.

Next, assess your risk tolerance to determine how much investment risk you're comfortable with. Consider factors such as your investment timeframe, financial stability, and emotional temperament. This assessment will help you strike a balance between pursuing potential returns and mitigating risk, ensuring that your investment plan aligns with your comfort level.

With your goals and risk tolerance in mind, outline specific investment strategies and asset allocations that will help you achieve your objectives while managing risk effectively. For example, if your goal is long-term wealth accumulation and you have a high risk tolerance, you may opt for a more aggressive investment approach with a higher allocation to stocks. Conversely, if you're nearing retirement and prioritize capital preservation, a more conservative strategy with a greater focus on bonds may be appropriate.

Your investment plan should also consider factors such as diversification, asset allocation, and periodic portfolio rebalancing to ensure optimal risk management and performance. Diversification involves spreading your investments across different asset classes, industries, and geographic regions to reduce the impact of any single investment's performance on your overall portfolio. Diversifying your portfolio across various asset classes is a fundamental strategy for mitigating risk and optimizing returns in your investment strategy. By spreading your investments across different asset classes, you reduce the impact of any single investment's performance on your overall portfolio, thus enhancing its resilience and potential for long-term growth.

Asset allocation involves strategically distributing your investments among different asset classes based on your financial goals, risk tolerance, and investment timeframe. Periodic portfolio rebalancing involves realigning your portfolio back to its target asset allocation to maintain risk levels and ensure that it remains aligned with your goals.

By crafting a personalized investment plan that addresses your financial goals, risk tolerance, and investment preferences, you can navigate the complexities of the financial markets with confidence and clarity. This plan provides a structured framework for making investment decisions and staying on track towards achieving your long-term financial objectives.

Check this out: A balanced portfolio may include a mix of stocks, bonds, real estate, and alternative investments, each offering unique risk-return profiles and diversification benefits. Stocks provide the potential for growth but come with higher volatility, while bonds offer stability and income with lower risk. Real estate investments can provide inflation protection and diversification benefits, while alternative investments such as commodities or private equity offer opportunities for further diversification and potential returns.

By diversifying your portfolio across these asset classes, you can achieve a well-rounded approach to wealth accumulation that balances potential returns with risk mitigation. During periods of market volatility or economic uncertainty, certain asset classes may perform better than others, helping to offset losses in other areas of your portfolio.

Moreover, diversification allows you to capture the benefits of different market cycles and investment opportunities, reducing the reliance on any single asset class to drive portfolio performance. This approach helps to smooth out investment returns over time and reduce the overall volatility of your portfolio, thereby enhancing its stability and sustainability.

Diversifying your portfolio across various asset classes is a key strategy for managing risk and optimizing returns in your investment strategy. By spreading your investments across different asset classes with unique risk-return profiles, you can build a well-balanced portfolio that is better positioned to weather market fluctuations and achieve your long-term financial goals.

Chapter Summary

Developing an investment strategy is a fundamental aspect of personal finance and investing. By setting clear financial goals, assessing your risk tolerance, and creating a personalized investment plan, you can navigate the complexities of the financial markets with confidence and clarity. Remember, smart money moves are not just about making investments; they are about securing your financial future and achieving your dreams.

Whether you're saving for retirement, planning for a major purchase, or building wealth over the long term, having a well-thought-out investment strategy is key to realizing your financial aspirations.

So, take the time to understand your goals, evaluate your risk tolerance, and craft a plan that aligns with your objectives. With diligence, patience, and informed decision-making, you can pave the way to financial success and turn your dreams into reality.

PRACTICAL INVESTMENT TECHNIQUES

This chapter introduces readers to various investment strategies that can be employed by individuals to enhance their investment portfolios. It begins by explaining the concept of dollar-cost averaging, a technique that allows investors to mitigate market volatility by investing a fixed amount of money at regular intervals, regardless of the market's performance. The chapter then delves into value investing, teaching readers how to identify undervalued assets that have the potential for significant growth. Growth investing is discussed next, with a focus on investing in companies that have strong potential for future earnings growth. Lastly, the chapter covers dividend investing, explaining how to create passive income streams by investing in dividend-paying stocks. Each section provides practical examples, illustrating how these techniques can be applied in real-world scenarios.

Dollar-Cost Averaging: Smoothing Out Market Volatility

Dollar-cost averaging is an investment strategy designed to reduce the impact of volatility in the stock market. It involves investing a fixed amount of money at regular intervals, such as monthly or quarterly, into a particular investment or portfolio, regardless of the asset's price at each interval. Here's how it works and why it's beneficial:

- **Regular Investment:** Instead of trying to time the market to buy at the lowest point, investors commit to investing a predetermined amount of money at set times. For example, an investor might decide to invest $500 into a mutual fund every month.
- **Mitigating Volatility:** By consistently investing the same amount of money, investors purchase more shares when prices are low and fewer shares when prices are high. This can mitigate the risk of investing a large amount of money at an inopportune time when prices are at their peak.
- **Market Performance Irrelevance:** The strategy does not require investors to predict market movements or performance. Since the investment occurs regardless of market conditions, it reduces the emotional stress associated with trying to time the market.
- **Compounding Benefits:** Over time, dollar-cost averaging can help investors build a substantial portfolio. As the number of shares accumulates, the potential for growth and compounding increases, especially if dividends are reinvested.
- **Suitability for Beginners and Long-term Investors:** This approach is particularly suitable for beginners or those who are risk-averse, as it simplifies the investment process and encourages a long-term perspective, which is often associated with reduced risk and improved investment outcomes.

In summary, dollar-cost averaging is a strategy that allows investors to take part in the market while potentially lowering the risks associated with market volatility. It promotes disciplined investing and can lead to wealth accumulation over the long term, making it a popular choice for individuals with a regular income who are looking to grow their investments in a relatively passive and steady manner.

Value Investing: Identifying Undervalued Assets

Value investing is a strategy that involves identifying and purchasing securities that appear underpriced by some form of fundamental analysis. Here's an overview of how the chapter might approach teaching readers about value investing:

Value investing is the investment strategy known for being promoted by legendary investors like Benjamin Graham and Warren Buffett. It is based on the principle of purchasing stocks that are trading for less than their intrinsic or true value, offering a margin of safety. This discrepancy between the market price and the intrinsic value is what provides the potential for profit. To identify these undervalued stocks, investors engage in thorough financial analysis, examining a company's fundamentals such as earnings, dividends, assets, and liabilities, alongside its business model and industry position. The goal is to find stocks that are not just cheap, but undervalued relative to their actual financial worth and future earning potential.

This method requires patience, as value stocks may take time to appreciate, and a contrarian mindset, as it often involves buying when others are selling and vice versa. Through this strategy, investors aim to build a portfolio of high-quality companies with robust prospects that are currently undervalued by the market, seeking to achieve superior long-term returns.

Stocks that are trading below their intrinsic value can occur for several reasons such as market overreaction, company-specific issues, or general sector unpopularity. It is important for you to dig deeper into companies that might be overlooked, misunderstood, or operating in sectors currently out of favor with most investors. Applying financial ratios and analysis effectively involves a systematic approach to evaluate and compare the financial health, performance, and valuation of companies.

Here's how you can do this:

- Collect Financial Data: Start by gathering the relevant financial information from a company's financial statements: the income statement, balance sheet, and cash flow statement. This data will form the basis of your analysis.
- Calculate Key Financial Ratios: Use the financial data to calculate ratios that will help assess the company's profitability, liquidity, solvency, and valuation. Important ratios include:
  - Profitability Ratios such as Net Profit Margin (Net Income/Revenue) and Return on Equity (Net Income/Shareholder's Equity) to evaluate how efficiently a company is generating profits.
  - Liquidity Ratios like the Current Ratio (Current Assets/Current Liabilities) and Quick Ratio (Liquid Assets/Current Liabilities) to assess the company's ability to meet short-term obligations.
  - Solvency Ratios such as the Debt-to-Equity Ratio (Total Debt/Total Equity) to understand the company's debt levels relative to its equity.
  - Valuation Ratios like the Price-to-Earnings (P/E) Ratio (Market Price per Share/Earnings per Share) and Price-to-Book (P/B) Ratio (Market Price per Share/Book Value per Share) to determine if the stock is overvalued or undervalued compared to its earnings and assets.
- Benchmark Against Industry Standards: Compare the calculated ratios to industry averages or direct competitors to gauge the company's performance relative to its peers. This comparison can help identify strengths and weaknesses and determine

whether the company stands out in its sector.

- Analyze Trends: Look at how these ratios have changed over time to identify any trends, improvements, or deteriorations in the company's financial health and performance. Consistent improvement in profitability or reduction in debt levels can be a positive sign, while declining margins or increasing debt may warrant caution.

- Consider Contextual Factors: Financial ratios should not be analyzed in isolation. Consider the broader economic environment, industry conditions, and company-specific factors such as management changes, new product launches, or regulatory changes that could impact the company's future performance.

- Make Informed Decisions: Use the insights gained from this analysis to make informed investment decisions. If the financial ratios and analysis indicate that a company is financially healthy, undervalued by the market, and has strong prospects, it may be a worthwhile investment opportunity. Conversely, if the analysis reveals overvaluation or financial instability, it might be wise to avoid investing in the company.

- Continuous Monitoring: Financial analysis is not a one-time task. Continuously monitor the financial health and performance of the company through regular updates to the financial ratios and by staying informed about any significant changes in the company or its industry.

By applying financial ratios and analysis effectively, investors can gain a deeper understanding of a company's financial position and make more informed decisions about their investments. Key tools include the price-to-earnings (P/E) ratio, which can indicate whether a stock is trading at a lower price relative to its earnings compared to peers, and the price-to-book (P/B) ratio, which helps assess whether a company's market price fairly reflects its book value. Additional metrics, like the debt-to-equity ratio and free cash flow, provide insight into a company's financial health and operational efficiency. By understanding and applying these analytical tools, investors can identify undervalued stocks that may offer significant upside potential once their true value is recognized by the market.

The margin of safety is a fundamental principle in value investing that acts as a protective buffer between the market price of a stock and its calculated intrinsic value. This concept, essential for reducing investment risk, was popularized by Benjamin Graham, a pioneer of value investing. The intrinsic value of a stock is determined through fundamental analysis, which includes evaluating a company's financial health, competitive advantages, and future earnings potential.

The margin of safety comes into play when an investor purchases a stock at a price significantly lower than its intrinsic value. This difference provides a "safety net" that helps protect the investor from losing money, particularly if there are errors in the intrinsic value calculation or if unexpected market downturns occur. The greater the margin of safety, the lower the risk of incurring a loss on the investment.

For example, if an investor calculates the intrinsic value of a stock to be $100 but can purchase it for $70, the $30 difference represents the margin of safety. This gap allows room for errors in the investor's analysis or for unforeseen events that might negatively impact the stock's value. By only investing in securities that meet this criterion, investors can minimize potential losses while increasing the likelihood of profitable investments, even in volatile or uncertain markets.

Value investing is fundamentally a long-term investment strategy that prioritizes buying stocks trading below their intrinsic value and holding them until their market price reflects their true worth. Here we emphasize the critical role of patience in value investing, as undervalued stocks do not always correct their price discrepancies immediately. Market inefficiencies, investor sentiments, and external economic factors can cause a stock to remain undervalued for extended periods.

Investors adopting this strategy should brace themselves for potential delays and remain focused on the eventual realization of the stock's intrinsic value, rather than getting swayed by short-term market fluctuations. This patience allows the investor to benefit from full value correction over time, capital appreciation, and dividends contributing to substantial long-term gains.

It is important for investors to resist the temptation to react to short-term market movements and instead maintain a disciplined approach to their investments. By doing so, they avoid making impulsive decisions based on market volatility and can better adhere to their investment thesis, which is based on thorough research and analysis of the company's fundamentals. This long-term perspective is essential in value investing, as it provides the time needed for the market to recognize the true value of the undervalued stocks and for the investment to reach its potential profitability.

In addressing the risks and considerations of value investing, it is important to point out that despite its potential for substantial returns, value investing is not without its challenges and pitfalls. One of the primary risks involved is the concept of value traps. These are stocks that appear to be undervalued based on traditional metrics but are cheap for valid reasons, such as significant underlying problems within the company or industry. These issues could include declining revenue, obsolete technology, poor management, or structural industry declines.

It would be amiss not to stress the importance of thorough research and due diligence to distinguish genuine undervalued opportunities from value traps. Investors are encouraged to look beyond surface-level financial metrics and delve deeper into the company's operations, competitive positioning, industry trends, and future growth prospects. This includes analyzing the company's earnings reports, understanding its business model, assessing the competence of its management team, and evaluating the health and outlook of the industry it operates in.

Recall what we learned in previous chapters about the importance of diversification to mitigate the risks associated with value investing. By spreading investments across various sectors and companies, investors can reduce the impact of a poor performing investment on their overall portfolio.

The necessity of having a clear exit strategy in investing is crucial, especially in value investing, where patience is a key component. An exit strategy is a pre-determined plan that specifies the conditions under which an investor decides to sell their holdings in a stock. This plan is essential to mitigate losses and realize profits at the right time. The discipline to adhere to this strategy helps investors avoid the common pitfall of holding onto losing investments due to emotional attachment or the unfounded hope that the stocks will eventually recover, a scenario known as "falling in love with your stocks."

Without a clear exit strategy, investors may cling to underperforming stocks for too long, waiting for a turnaround that may never come, which can lead to significant losses. Conversely, they might also sell their successful investments too early, missing out on potential further gains. A well-defined exit strategy should consider several factors, including specific financial goals, risk tolerance, market conditions, and changes in the fundamentals of the company or industry that originally justified the investment.

By establishing clear criteria for selling — such as reaching a certain price target, a specified rate of return, or upon recognizing a fundamental deterioration in the company's outlook — investors can remove emotion from the decision-making process. This approach promotes disciplined investing, helps manage risk, and can lead to more consistent investment outcomes.

Finally, the chapter would remind investors that value investing requires patience and a long-term perspective, as undervalued stocks may take time to appreciate, and premature selling could result in missed opportunities for significant growth.

CASE STUDY 1

Warren Buffet's Coca-Cola Investment

Background:

Warren Buffett, the chairperson and CEO of Berkshire Hathaway, is one of the most successful investors in history, largely due to his value investing approach. One of his most notable investments was in The Coca-Cola Company during the late 1980s.

Investment Decision:

In 1988, Buffett began purchasing shares of Coca-Cola, eventually accumulating about 7% of the company for Berkshire Hathaway. This move came after a significant market crash in 1987 and during a period when consumer goods companies were not the market's favorites. However, Buffett saw a unique opportunity in Coca-Cola, influenced by several key factors:

- **Brand Strength and Consumer Loyalty:** Buffett recognized Coca-Cola's brand as one of the most valuable and recognizable in the world, contributing to significant competitive moat. He understood the power of brand loyalty, which ensured consistent consumer demand and pricing power.
- **Global Reach and Market Penetration:** Despite its already massive global presence, Buffett saw further growth potential, especially in emerging markets. He believed Coca-Cola's international expansion strategies could lead to substantial long-term growth.
- **Financial Health:** Buffett examined Coca-Cola's financial statements and was impressed by the company's profitability, strong free cash flow, and solid balance

sheet. These factors indicated a healthy, well-run company capable of sustaining growth and returning value to shareholders.

- **Historical Performance and Valuation:** By the late 1980s, despite its strong fundamentals, Coca-Cola's stock was trading at a price that Buffett considered undervalued, particularly in light of its earnings potential and global market opportunities. This discrepancy presented the margin of safety Buffett looks for in investments.

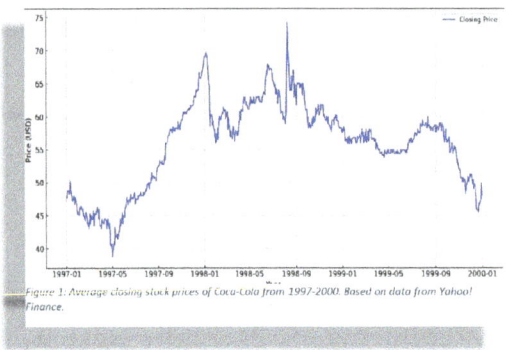

Figure 1: Average closing stock prices of Coca-Cola from 1997-2000. Based on data from Yahoo! Finance.

Outcome:

Buffett's investment in Coca-Cola is one of the most successful in investment history. Since 1988, the value of Berkshire Hathaway's holdings in Coca-Cola has grown exponentially, providing substantial dividends and capital appreciation. This investment has become a textbook example of value investing, demonstrating the importance of patience, long-term thinking, and conviction in one's analysis.

Lessons Learned:

- **Understand Intrinsic Value:** Buffett's strategy hinges on identifying companies trading below their intrinsic value but with strong fundamentals and growth prospects.
- **Look for Competitive Advantages:** Companies with

a strong competitive moat, like Coca-Cola's brand and market reach, can sustain profits and fend off competition over the long term.

- **Assess Global Potential:** Buffett saw beyond the current market conditions and understood Coca-Cola's potential for international expansion.
- **Patience Pays Off:** Value investing requires patience; undervalued stocks may take time to reach their true potential.
- **Stick to Your Principles:** Despite market fluctuations and trends, sticking to a well-researched investment thesis can lead to significant rewards.

Buffett's investment in Coca-Cola underscores the effectiveness of value investing principles when applied diligently and patiently, emphasizing the importance of understanding a company's intrinsic value and growth potential beyond prevailing market sentiments.

Growth Investing: Capitalizing on Future Potential

Growth investing is an investment strategy that focuses on acquiring stocks of companies expected to grow at an above-average rate compared to their industry or the overall market. This approach is particularly focused on investing in companies with strong potential for future earnings growth. Here's how growth investing works and the key aspects that define this strategy:

- Focus on Future Potential: Growth investing focuses on companies with high potential for future growth, even if they're not currently undervalued. Unlike value investing, which seeks out cheap stocks based on current financials, growth investing looks for firms that may be expensive now but are expected to grow significantly in terms of earnings, revenue, or cash flow.

- **Company Characteristics:** Growth investors search for companies with special products, strong brands, advanced technology, or new market access, as these traits can lead to faster sales and profit increases compared to competitors.

- **Sector and Industry Trends:** Growth investors typically target rapidly growing sectors like technology, biotech, renewable energy, or e-commerce, as these areas are more likely to have companies with high growth potential.

- **Long-term Investment:** Growth stocks may be riskier and more volatile than typical stocks, but the approach often focuses on long-term investing. Investors pay more for these stocks, hoping that the company's growth will eventually result in significant long-term profits.

- **Reinvestment of Earnings:** Companies ideal for growth investing usually put their profits back into the business instead of distributing dividends. They might invest in research and development, expansion, or other efforts to boost growth and capture a larger market share.

- **Risk and Volatility:** Growth investing is riskier and can change a lot in value compared to other methods. This is because growth stocks cost more compared to what they currently earn, making them react more to market changes and bad news. But the chance for big profits may make these risks worth it for some investors.

- **Performance Evaluation:** Investors in growth investing watch the company's earnings, revenue growth, and plans for expansion closely to make sure they still fit the growth investment profile.

Growth investing involves searching for and investing in companies that have outstanding potential for growth, even if their current prices seem high. Investors who use this strategy are not as interested in traditional signs that a stock is undervalued. Instead, they focus on the company's future ability to increase earnings and become dominant in the market. They are willing to accept more risk and deal with more ups and downs in stock prices for the chance of getting higher returns over the long term.

Dividend Investing: Generating Passive Income Streams

Dividend investing is a strategy focused on generating income through stocks that pay dividends. Dividends are portions of a company's earnings that are paid out to shareholders on a regular basis, typically quarterly. This approach to investing is particularly appealing to those looking to receive a steady income stream from their investments, such as retirees or income-focused investors. Here's an overview of dividend investing and how it can create passive income streams:

Selection of Dividend-Paying Stocks: Investors look for companies that have a history of paying consistent and, ideally, increasing dividends. These companies are often well-established and financially stable, with a strong track record of profitability and cash flow. Industries like utilities, consumer goods, and real estate (through Real Estate Investment Trusts, or REITs) are known for having many dividend-paying companies.

Income Generation: The primary goal of dividend investing is to generate income. By holding shares of dividend-paying companies, investors receive regular dividend payments. These payments can provide a steady income stream separate from any stock price movements, which can be particularly valuable during market downturns or for investors who need regular income.

Reinvestment: Investors may choose to reinvest their dividends to purchase more shares of the stock, a process known as dividend reinvestment. This can lead to compounding growth, as the additional shares acquired will also generate dividends, which can then be used to buy even more shares.

Diversification: Investing in a diversified portfolio of dividend-paying stocks can help spread risk. Different sectors and industries react differently to economic conditions, so diversification can provide a more stable overall income stream.

Tax Considerations: Dividend income is subject to taxation, but the tax rate can vary based on the type of dividend (qualified vs. non-qualified) and the investor's tax bracket. Understanding these tax implications is crucial for effectively managing the income generated from dividends.

Long-term Growth Potential: While the primary focus of dividend investing is income, there can also be an opportunity for capital appreciation. If the selected companies grow over time, the value of the shares can increase, providing investors with both income and growth.

Risk Management: Although dividend investing is considered less risky than investing in non-dividend-paying stocks, there are still risks involved, including the potential for companies to reduce or eliminate their dividend payments in tough economic times. Therefore, thorough research and ongoing monitoring of the investment are essential.

Dividend investing is about choosing companies that regularly pay dividends to generate a steady source of income. This strategy is ideal for investors seeking passive income or those who prefer a safer, more conservative approach to investing. By putting money into a variety of dividend-paying stocks, investors can enjoy regular income while also having the opportunity for the value of their investments to grow. This approach is less risky compared to investing in growth-oriented stocks, which can fluctuate more in price.

Chapter Summary

This chapter covers different investment strategies to help individuals enhance their portfolios. It starts with dollar-cost averaging, a method to lessen market volatility effects by investing a fixed sum regularly. It's a suitable strategy for beginners and promotes long-term investment.

Next, the chapter explores value investing, which involves identifying undervalued assets through fundamental analysis. This strategy, endorsed by renowned investors like Benjamin Graham and Warren Buffett, requires patience and a detailed examination of a company's financials and market position.

Growth investing is then discussed, highlighting the approach of investing in companies expected to grow significantly. This strategy focuses on firms with unique products or services, strong brands, or new market access, despite their current high valuations.

Finally, dividend investing is examined. This strategy involves investing in companies that regularly pay dividends, providing a steady income stream. It's particularly appealing for those seeking passive income or a conservative investment approach.

NAVIGATING
MARKET TRENDS

In this chapter, you will learn how to interpret and respond to market trends and economic indicators effectively. The chapter begins with an overview of market analysis, including how to understand key economic indicators like GDP, unemployment rates, and inflation. It then addresses the psychological aspects of investing, introducing the concept of behavioral finance and highlighting common emotional biases that can adversely affect investment decisions. The chapter concludes with a discussion on the merits and pitfalls of attempting to time the market versus maintaining a long-term investment strategy, helping you understand the importance of time in the market over timing the market.

Market Analysis: Understanding Economic Indicators and Trends

We can start by discussing how to analyze the market by looking at important economic indicators such as GDP (Gross Domestic Product), unemployment rates, and inflation. These indicators help investors understand the overall health of the economy, which can influence investment decisions.

GDP is the total monetary or market value of all the finished goods and services produced within a country's borders in a specific time period. It acts as a comprehensive scorecard of a country's economic health. GDP includes all private and public consumption, government outlays, investments, additions to private inventories, paid-in construction costs, and the foreign balance of trade (exports are added, imports are subtracted).

GDP can be calculated using three approaches: the production (or output) approach, the income approach, and the expenditure approach. Each offers a unique perspective but should theoretically result in the same total. GDP is a critical data point for economists and policymakers as it provides a broad overview of the state of an economy and is often used to compare the economic performance of different countries or regions.

If the GDP is growing, it often means the economy is strong, which can be good for stocks. If unemployment rates are falling, it suggests more people are finding jobs, leading to increased consumer spending and potentially positive effects on the stock market. On the other hand, high inflation rates can erode purchasing power and affect consumer spending, which may negatively impact certain investments.

Let's say the latest report shows that GDP has increased by 3% from the previous quarter, indicating economic growth. At the same time, unemployment rates have decreased from 6% to 4%, suggesting more people are employed and likely to spend more. However, inflation has also risen to 5% from 2%. While the growth in GDP and decrease in unemployment are positive signs for the economy and could lead to a rise in stock prices, the increase in inflation could signal rising costs and lower consumer spending power, potentially harming some investments. Investors might use this information to adjust their portfolios, by investing in sectors that benefit from economic growth or by avoiding areas that are negatively impacted by high inflation.

The story of the Great Inflation begins in the late 1960s and extends through the early 1980s, a period that stands out as one of the most challenging economic times in U.S. history. The roots of the problem were multifaceted, involving a combination of domestic policy decisions and international events.

The problem started during the presidency of Lyndon B. Johnson, who introduced his "Great Society" social programs. These initiatives, alongside the escalating costs of the Vietnam War, led to increased government spending without equivalent tax increases, resulting in budget deficits. At the same time, the Federal Reserve, under the leadership of then-Chairman William McChesney Martin and later Arthur Burns, pursued a policy of low interest rates, aiming to support full employment.

The oil shocks of the 1970s further exacerbated the situation. OPEC (Organization of Petroleum Exporting Countries) imposed an oil embargo in 1973 due to political tensions, which caused oil prices to quadruple. A second oil crisis followed in 1979, stemming from the Iranian Revolution. These events led to a dramatic increase in the price of gasoline and heating oil, affecting almost every aspect of American life.

The impacts of the Great Inflation were widespread and deeply felt. As prices soared, the purchasing power of the American dollar plummeted, eroding savings and fixed incomes. The cost of living skyrocketed, making everyday goods and services unaffordable for many Americans. Unemployment rates also rose, as businesses struggled with higher production costs and reduced consumer spending.

This period of "stagflation" — a term coined to describe the unusual combination of high inflation and high unemployment — challenged the prevailing economic theories of the time, which held that inflation and unemployment moved in opposite directions.

The resolution came with the appointment of Paul Volcker as the Chairman of the Federal Reserve in 1979. Recognizing the severity of the inflation problem, Volcker implemented a series of drastic measures. He significantly raised the federal funds rate, which in turn increased interest rates across the board, making borrowing more expensive. His aim was to reduce the money supply and, consequently, to tame inflation.

These policies, while successful in reducing inflation, also led to a deep recession in the early 1980s. Unemployment reached its highest level since the Great Depression, and many businesses went bankrupt. However, the tough measures were seen as necessary to reset the economy.

By the mid-1980s, inflation had been significantly reduced, setting the stage for a period of economic growth and stability. The Great Inflation and its resolution left a lasting impact on economic policy and the role of central banks in managing economies. The era underscored the importance of disciplined fiscal and monetary policies and reshaped the Federal Reserve's approach to inflation, prioritizing price stability as a fundamental goal.

Behavioral Finance: Overcoming Emotional Biases in Decision-Making

Now, it's important to turn our attention to the psychological aspects of investing, specifically through the lens of behavioral finance. This area of study delves into how psychological factors and inherent biases can shape the investment choices made by individuals. Unlike traditional finance theories that assume people make rational decisions, behavioral finance recognizes that investors often make decisions based on emotions and cognitive biases.

For example, one common bias is 'overconfidence,' where investors overestimate their knowledge and ability to predict market movements, often leading to riskier investment choices. Another example is 'herd behavior,' where investors follow the actions of a majority, even if those actions contradict their own analysis or the fundamentals of the market.

Understanding behavioral finance helps investors recognize and mitigate these biases to make more informed and objective decisions, leading to better investment outcomes. It underscores the complexity of financial decision-making and the need for a more nuanced approach that considers the human elements influencing market dynamics.

Behavioral finance points out that investors frequently make decisions based on emotion rather than logic, leading to irrational behaviors. A prevalent emotional bias is the 'confirmation bias,' where individuals look for and give more weight to information that supports their existing opinions, while disregarding or undervaluing evidence that refutes them.

For instance, suppose Ken is heavily invested in the stock of a particular tech company because he believes it has robust growth potential. Despite recent reports indicating significant financial problems within the company and a declining market for its products, Ken focuses only on positive news or analyses that support the company's future success. He disregards the negative reports as anomalies or misunderstandings. As a result, Ken continues to hold or even increase his investment based on his biased collection of information, leading to potential monetary loss when the company's stock value continues to decline.

This example illustrates how confirmation bias can cloud judgment and lead to decisions that aren't supported by a full range of facts, highlighting the importance of considering diverse viewpoints and data in investment decision-making.

The 'loss aversion' bias is a psychological tendency where the fear of losing money is stronger than the pleasure of making an equivalent amount. This bias can significantly impact investor behavior, particularly during market downturns.

For example, consider an investor named Maria who has invested in a variety of stocks. When the market begins to drop, Maria, driven by a strong fear of losing her investment, quickly sells off her stocks to avoid further losses. This reaction is a direct result of her loss aversion bias; she's so focused on avoiding losses that she disregards the potential long-term gains that could arise if she held onto her stocks.

However, if the market recovers after Maria has sold her stocks, she misses out on the rebound and the potential profits she could have earned had she kept her investments. By reacting impulsively to short-term market fluctuations and acting out of fear, Maria realizes unnecessary losses and loses the opportunity for future gains.

This example illustrates how loss aversion can lead investors to make decisions that are not in their best long-term financial interest. It highlights the importance of maintaining a long-term perspective and resisting the urge to make hasty decisions based on short-term market movements.

Hopefully by now, you have come to understand how emotions and psychological biases can negatively impact their investment strategies and outcomes. By recognizing these biases, investors can work to minimize their influence and make more informed, rational investment decisions.

Timing the Market vs. Time in the Market: The Debate Unveiled

There is a stark difference between attempting to predict market movements (timing the market) and adhering to a long-term investment approach (time in the market). Here, we'll examine the advantages and drawbacks of each method to assist readers in understanding why remaining invested is more beneficial than attempting to forecast market changes.

One of the most illustrative periods in American economic history regarding the perils and pitfalls of attempting to time the market is the dot-com bubble of the late 1990s and early 2000s. This era saw a rapid rise in equity markets fueled by investments in internet-based companies, despite many of these firms lacking sustainable business models or even revenues.

During the dot-com boom, investors were drawn to the promising tech sector, enticed by the prospect of substantial returns. As stock prices surged, the merit seen in attempting to time the market was the potential for massive gains, with stories of overnight millionaires becoming a powerful lure. Many investors believed they could predict the continuing rise of the market and cash out before any downturn.

However, the pitfalls of this strategy were sharply exposed when the bubble burst in the early 2000s. The difficulty of accurately predicting market movements became apparent as the stock market's volatility and the influence of unforeseeable events, such as changes in investor sentiment or economic policies, led to dramatic losses for those trying to time their exit.

Many investors sold their positions in other sectors to invest more in technology stocks at what turned out to be peak prices. When the market corrected, those who had attempted to time the peak were left with significant losses. Conversely, investors who exited the market early to avoid a crash missed out on the initial gains as the market climbed higher than most had predicted. Moreover, the frequent trading associated with market timing led to higher transaction costs and capital gains taxes, further eroding returns for individual investors.

The dot-com bust highlighted the advantages of a long-term investment strategy. Investors who maintained diversified portfolios and resisted the urge to chase the tech bubble's highs typically experienced less volatility and saw their investments recover more quickly after the crash. This period in economic history serves as a stark reminder of the risks associated with trying to time the market and underscores the importance of being in the market, rather than attempting to predict its movements.

Attempting to time the market involves making investment decisions based on predictions of future market movements. The merit of this approach is the potential for high returns if the investor correctly predicts market highs and lows. However, the pitfalls are significant: it's extremely difficult to predict market movements consistently due to the market's volatility and the influence of unforeseeable events. This strategy can lead to missed opportunities, as investors might exit the market too early or re-enter too late, missing periods of substantial gains. Moreover, frequent trading can incur higher costs and taxes.

Conversely, maintaining a long-term investment strategy involves investing with a long-term perspective, typically ignoring short-term market fluctuations. The merits of this approach include the potential for compound returns over time, reduced impact of short-term volatility, and lower transaction costs due to less frequent trading. While the pitfall of long-term investing is that it requires patience and the ability to endure periods of market downturn without panic selling, it leads to more favorable outcomes for many investors.

A pivotal moment in American economic history that illustrates the benefits of maintaining a long-term investment strategy is the Great Recession, which spanned from December 2007 to June 2009. This period was marked by a significant decline in economic activity across markets worldwide, leading to a sharp drop in stock prices and severe impacts on investor confidence.

Before the recession, many investors enjoyed years of market growth. However, as the crisis unfolded, the stock market plummeted, presenting a real test of investors' resolve. Those with a long-term perspective, however, saw the merits of their approach. Despite the market's downturn, they understood the benefits of compound returns over time, recognizing that the market has historically trended upward despite short-term fluctuations.

By not capitulating to the panic that led many to sell off their investments at low prices, long-term investors minimized the impact of short-term volatility. Furthermore, by maintaining their investment positions, they incurred fewer transaction costs, avoiding the fees and taxes associated with frequent trading, which can erode investment returns.

However, this strategy was not without its challenges. The primary pitfall of long-term investing, particularly evident during the Great Recession, was the requirement for patience and the ability to endure prolonged market downturns. Watching the value of their portfolios decline, long-term investors needed to resist the urge to sell and lock in losses. This period was a true test of the investors' ability to stick to their investment principles despite widespread fear and uncertainty.

The resolution and aftermath of the Great Recession highlighted the advantages of a long-term investment strategy. Investors who held onto their assets and continued to invest throughout the downturn often saw significant recoveries in their portfolio values as the market rebounded in the following years. By 2013, the stock market had recovered all the losses incurred during the recession and continued to climb, rewarding those who remained invested with considerable gains.

The Great Recession serves as a profound lesson in the resilience required for long-term investing. It underscores the importance of maintaining a strategic focus, resisting the reactionary impulses prompted by market downturns, and trusting in the historical trend of market recovery. For many, this era reinforced the wisdom of a long-term outlook and the potential for favorable outcomes, despite the inevitable ebb and flow of the market's fortunes.

Staying invested for a long time is usually more beneficial than trying to guess the best moments to buy or sell. Historically, people who keep their money in the market for longer usually see better results than those who try to jump in and out at the "right" times. While it might be tempting to try to time the market, being patient and sticking to a long-term investing strategy often works out better.

Chapter Summary

This chapter teaches readers how to understand and react to market trends and economic signals effectively. It begins with an explanation of market analysis, focusing on crucial economic indicators like GDP, unemployment rates, and inflation, and how they reflect the overall health of the economy. Understanding these can help investors make informed decisions.

Next, the chapter moves into the psychological realm of investing, introducing behavioral finance. It discusses how emotional biases, such as overconfidence and loss aversion, can lead to poor investment decisions. By understanding these biases, investors can make more objective and informed choices.

Finally, the chapter debates the merits and challenges of market timing versus long-term investing. It makes clear that while market timing might appear attractive, it's usually less effective than a patient, long-term approach. Historical examples demonstrate that staying invested over the long term typically yields better returns, despite the temptations and pitfalls of trying to time market entries and exits.

In simple terms, the chapter advises that it's better to stay invested and ride out market fluctuations rather than trying to predict market movements, which can lead to missed opportunities and higher costs.

ADVANCED INVESTMENT STRATEGIES

Here, we shall delve into more sophisticated investment strategies for those who are ready to take their investment to the next level. It starts with an introduction to options trading, explaining the basics and how options can be used for both speculation and risk management. The chapter then transitions into real estate investing, covering topics such as property ownership, rental income, and the potential tax benefits of real estate investments. Retirement planning is the last section, where readers are guided through various strategies to build a secure financial future, including understanding several types of retirement accounts and how to plan for retirement savings.

Options Trading: Leveraging Derivatives for Risk Management and Speculation

Options trading involves buying and selling options, which are financial contracts that give the buyer the right, but not the obligation, to buy or sell an underlying asset at a specified price (known as the strike price) before a certain date (the expiration date). Options are used for various purposes, including speculation and risk management.

Call Options: Buying a call option gives you the right to _purchase_ the underlying asset at the strike price before the expiration date. If you believe the price of the asset will go up, you might buy a call option to profit from the price increase.

Put Options: Buying a put option gives you the right to _sell_ the underlying asset at the strike price before the expiration date. If you believe the price of the asset will go down, you might buy a put option to profit from the price decrease.

Options are bought and sold on options exchanges, like how stocks are traded. Each option contract typically represents 100 shares of the underlying asset, although the asset could be indexes or futures contracts as well.

Investors use options for speculation when they anticipate the market moving in a particular direction. For example, if an investor expects a stock's price to rise, they might buy call options to leverage their position. If the stock's price rises above the strike price, the investor can exercise the option to buy the stock at a lower price, then sell it at the current market price, capturing the difference as profit.

Conversely, if an investor expects a stock's price to fall, they might buy put options. If the stock's price falls below the strike price, the investor can exercise the option to sell the stock at a higher price than its current market price, again capturing the difference as profit.

Options can also be used for hedging, which is a way to manage risk. For instance, if you own shares of a company and are concerned about a short-term decrease in the stock price, you can buy put options as a form of insurance. If the stock price falls, your loss on the stock is offset by gains on the put options.

Similarly, if you have sold stocks short (betting that the price will fall), you could buy call options to protect against unexpected price increases. If the stock price rises, the loss on the short position could be offset by gains from the call options.

Sarah and Jennifer are two investors who are looking to manage risks associated with their investments in different scenarios.

Sarah owns 100 shares of TechCo, a tech company currently trading at $50 per share. She is optimistic about the company's long-term growth but is concerned about potential short-term market volatility that could lead to a significant drop in the stock price.

To protect her investment, Sarah decides to use a hedging strategy by purchasing put options for TechCo with a strike price of $45, expiring in three months. The put options give her the right to sell her TechCo shares at $45, regardless of how low the market price may drop. She pays a premium (the cost of the option) of $2 per share, or $200 total for the 100 shares.

Two months later, the market experiences a downturn, and TechCo's stock falls to $40 per share. Thanks to her put options, Sarah can exercise her right to sell her shares at $45, despite the market price being $40. By using the put options as insurance, Sarah has effectively limited her loss to the premium she paid for the options ($200), rather than the $1,000 loss she would have faced without the hedge.

On the other hand, Jennifer has taken a different approach. She believes that TechCo's stock is overvalued and is poised for a decline. Therefore, she decides to short-sell 100 shares of TechCo at the current price of $50, betting that the price will fall.

However, Jennifer is also aware of the risks. If TechCo releases unexpectedly positive news, its stock price could surge, leading to significant losses on her short position. To hedge this risk, she buys call options for TechCo with a strike price of $55, expiring in three months, paying a premium of $2 per share, or $200 total.

Unexpectedly, TechCo announces a groundbreaking new product, and its stock price jumps to $60 per share. Jennifer faces a potential loss on her short position since she must buy back the shares at a much higher price than she sold them. However, because she owns call options, she can now buy TechCo shares at only $55 instead of the market price of $60. Her loss on the short position is mitigated by the gains from her call options.

In these examples, both Sarah and Jennifer used options to hedge against their investment risks. Sarah used put options to protect against a drop in the stock price of a company she owns shares in, while Jennifer used call options to protect against a rise in the stock price of a company she has shorted. By doing so, they were able to manage their risks effectively, demonstrating how options can be powerful tools for hedging in various investment scenarios.

Options trading offers flexibility for various strategies, including speculation and risk management. However, it's essential to remember that options trading can be complex and carries an elevated level of risk. It requires a good understanding of the market and the specific terms and conditions of the options contracts. Beginners should approach options trading with caution and consider seeking advice from financial advisors or experienced traders.

Real Estate Investing: Exploring Property Ownership and Rental Income

Real estate investing involves purchasing property to generate income or profit. This can include residential, commercial, or industrial properties. Here's an overview of the key aspects:

Property ownership in real estate investing means acquiring legal rights to a property. Investors can buy properties outright or finance them through loans. Owning property can provide investors with control over their investment, allowing them to make improvements, lease it out, or sell the property for profit.

One of the primary ways real estate investors make money is through rental income. This involves leasing out the property to tenants and collecting rent. The income generated from rent can cover the property's expenses, such as mortgage payments, property taxes, insurance, and maintenance. Ideally, there should be a positive cash flow, meaning the rental income exceeds the property's operating expenses. Rental properties can provide a steady source of income and can be particularly attractive during times of inflation when rental rates may increase.

In addition to rental income, real estate investments can also lead to profits through appreciation—the increase in the property's value over time. This can occur due to changes in the real estate market, improvements made to the property, or development in the surrounding area. When the property's value increases, investors can sell it for a profit.

Real estate investments offer various tax advantages that can increase profitability. These may include deductions for mortgage interest, property taxes, operating expenses, depreciation, and repairs. Depreciation allows investors to reduce their taxable income by accounting for the property's wear and tear over time. Additionally, if an investor sells a property that has increased in value, the capital gains may be taxed at a lower rate than regular income, especially if the property was held for over a year.

Real estate investing allows for leverage, meaning investors can use borrowed capital to increase the potential return of an investment. For example, an investor might use a mortgage to finance the purchase of a property with a small down payment and borrow the rest. This can amplify returns but also increases risk since the investor must keep up with loan payments.

While real estate investing can offer significant rewards, it also comes with risks. These can include market fluctuations, vacancies, non-paying tenants, and unexpected maintenance issues. Additionally, real estate is an illiquid asset, meaning it can take time to sell a property and access the invested capital.

In summary, real estate investing involves acquiring properties to generate rental income and potentially profit from appreciation. It offers benefits such as steady income, tax deductions, and the potential for high returns. However, like all investments, it requires careful research, management, and consideration of the associated risks and responsibilities.

Retirement Planning: Strategies for Building a Secure Financial Future

Retirement planning is the process of setting retirement income goals and deciding the necessary actions and decisions to achieve those goals. This involves identifying sources of income, estimating expenses, implementing a savings program, and managing assets. A well-structured retirement plan considers a range of factors, including the age at which you plan to retire, the lifestyle you expect to lead, and your financial situation.

401(k) and 403(b) Plans: These are employer-sponsored retirement savings plans. Employees can contribute a portion of their salary to these accounts, which are often tax-deferred until withdrawal in retirement. Many employers offer matching contributions to a certain percentage, which helps to grow retirement savings faster.

IRA (Individual Retirement Account): There are two main types of IRAs: Traditional and Roth. With a Traditional IRA, you may get tax deductions on your contributions depending on your income, but you'll pay taxes when you withdraw the money in retirement. Roth IRAs are funded with after-tax dollars, meaning withdrawals in retirement are tax-free, provided certain conditions are met.

SEP IRA and SIMPLE IRA: These are IRAs designed for self-employed individuals or small business owners. They allow for higher contribution limits than traditional IRAs but have specific rules and limitations.

Defined Benefit Plans: Also known as pension plans, these provide a specified monthly benefit at retirement, often based on salary and years of service.

We'll cover these types of investments in greater detail in the next chapter, so don't worry if you're not up to speed on how they work just yet.

So, how does one go about planning for retirement? Here's a few steps that can help you enjoy those "golden years":

- Estimate Your Retirement Needs: Start by estimating your annual retirement expenses. Consider your current expenses and think about how they might change in retirement. Experts often suggest you'll need around 70-90% of your pre-retirement income to maintain your standard of living.
- Calculate Your Income: Determine potential

retirement income from various sources, such as Social Security, pensions, investments, rental properties, and savings. Understand when each source becomes available; for example, you can start claiming Social Security benefits from age 62, but full retirement age may be later.

- Contribute Regularly: Take advantage of compounding interest by starting to save and invest as early as possible. Make regular contributions to your retirement accounts, and if possible, maximize your contributions to meet any limits set by the IRS.
- Invest Wisely: Diversify your investment portfolio to balance risk and return. Consider your risk tolerance and investment horizon when choosing your investments. As you approach retirement, you may want to shift towards more conservative investments to protect your savings.
- Plan for Healthcare Costs: Healthcare can be a significant expense in retirement. Consider investing in a health savings account (HSA) if you're eligible, and research your options for Medicare or supplemental insurance.
- Monitor and Adjust: Review your retirement plan regularly and adjust your savings and investments as needed. Life changes, such as marriage, having children, or changing jobs, can impact your retirement planning.
- Seek Professional Advice: Consider consulting with a financial advisor who can provide personalized advice based on your financial situation and retirement goals.

The FIRE method stands for Financial Independence, Retire Early. It's a movement that has gained popularity among many seeking to achieve financial freedom much earlier than traditional retirement ages. The core principle of FIRE is to live a frugal lifestyle, save a substantial portion of your income (typically around 50-70%), and invest aggressively to allow for early retirement.

Financial independence is a key concept in the FIRE method and in traditional retirement planning. It refers to the stage where you have accumulated enough assets—such as savings, investments, real estate, or other income-generating assets—that the income produced from these assets is sufficient to cover your living expenses for the near future, without the need to work full-time.

The idea is to reach a point where you are no longer financially dependent on a regular paycheck from employment to maintain your lifestyle. Instead, you rely on the passive income generated by your investments or the capital you have built up. This could come from various sources, including interest, dividends, rent from investment properties, or profits from other investments.

Achieving financial independence requires careful planning, aggressive saving, and prudent investing. It often involves living below one's means to increase the rate of savings, investing wisely to grow wealth, and carefully managing expenses to ensure that accumulated assets can sustain one's lifestyle indefinitely.

Financial independence in the context of the FIRE method and traditional retirement planning means having the financial security and freedom to make life decisions without being constrained by financial limitations. It provides the option to retire early, pursue hobbies, travel, or engage in other activities without the need to earn a salary to cover daily living costs.

The FIRE approach places a strong emphasis on saving and investing as key strategies to achieve early financial independence. Unlike traditional retirement planning, which might suggest saving 10-20% of one's income, the FIRE method advocates for a much more aggressive approach, often recommending that individuals save 50-70% of their income.

The idea is to significantly reduce your living expenses to increase the amount of income available to save and invest.

This often involves adopting a frugal lifestyle, minimizing unnecessary expenditures, and finding ways to increase income. The goal is to create a substantial gap between income and expenses, allowing for significant savings.

Saving alone isn't enough, though. The FIRE approach emphasizes investing these savings into various investment vehicles like 401(k)s, Individual Retirement Accounts (IRAs), stocks, bonds, real estate, and other income-generating assets. The aim is to put your money to work, earning a return that outpaces inflation and grows your wealth over time.

Retirement accounts often offer tax advantages that can enhance the growth of your investments. For example, money invested in a 401(k) or traditional IRA may grow tax-deferred, and contributions might reduce your taxable income. Roth IRAs, while funded with after-tax dollars, allow for tax-free growth and withdrawals in retirement, providing significant tax benefits over the long term.

The FIRE method relies heavily on the power of compound interest, where the returns on your investments generate their own returns. By saving and investing aggressively at an early age, you maximize the time your money has to grow, leveraging the compounding effect to build a substantial nest egg.

Properly diversifying your investment portfolio is another key aspect, and hopefully you've noticed, is a recurring theme. This involves spreading your investments across different asset classes to reduce risk while maximizing potential returns. Diversification can help protect your savings from market volatility and ensure more stable growth over time.

The saving and investing principle in the FIRE approach is about much more than just setting aside money for the future. It's about living below your means, aggressively saving a substantial portion of your income, and investing those savings wisely to build wealth rapidly. This enables individuals following the FIRE method to achieve financial independence and consider early retirement much sooner than traditional retirement planning might allow. While traditional retirement planning often targets retirement ages of 65 or later, FIRE aims to achieve retirement much earlier, sometimes as soon as in one's 30s or 40s. This requires more aggressive saving and investing strategies and often a more minimalist lifestyle.

FIRE practitioners must plan carefully for withdrawal strategies to ensure their savings last throughout their potentially longer retirement period. This includes considering withdrawal rates, tax implications, and market fluctuations, like standard retirement planning but with the added challenge of a longer timeframe.

The FIRE method is a more aggressive form of retirement planning that aims for financial independence and the possibility of early retirement. It shares many principles with traditional retirement planning, such as saving, investing, and expense management, but differs in its level of intensity and the early retirement goal. For those interested in the FIRE approach, it's important to adapt retirement planning strategies to fit the unique challenges and opportunities that retiring early presents. Remember, retirement planning is a long-term process. The earlier you start planning and saving, the better prepared you will be to enjoy a comfortable and secure

◆ ◆ ◆

CASE STUDY 2

Igniting the FIRE: Jay's Journey

from Geologist to Financial Independence...Almost.

Introduction:

Jay, a 30-year-old geologist, discovered the Financial Independence, Retire Early (FIRE) method amidst the rocks and sediment layers that dominated his daily life. Inspired by the concept of gaining financial freedom and retiring early, Jay embarked on a journey to reshape his financial landscape. This article explores Jay's path towards financial independence, the strategic steps he took, the pitfalls he encountered, and the crucial lessons he learned along the way.

Getting Started With The Fire Method:

Jay's journey began with a deep dive into his finances. He meticulously reviewed his income, expenses, and investment portfolio, establishing a clear picture of his financial health. Understanding the core of the FIRE method required Jay to adopt a frugal lifestyle, drastically cutting unnecessary expenses while maximizing his savings rate. He aimed to save and invest at least 50-70% of his income, adhering to the aggressive savings strategy advocated by FIRE enthusiasts.

Jay's initial plan included:
- Creating a detailed budget to track and control his spending.
- Setting up an emergency fund to cover unexpected expenses.
- Paying off high-interest debt to avoid wasteful interest payments.
- Increasing his income through side hustles and seeking promotions at work.
- Investing wisely in low-cost index funds and maximizing contributions to tax-advantaged

accounts like Roth IRAs and 401(k)s.

Jay focused on the power of compound interest and the importance of a diversified investment portfolio. He educated himself on tax-efficient investing and allocated his assets across various accounts to optimize returns and minimize taxes. Jay's investment strategy emphasized long-term growth, patience, and consistency. He automated his savings and investments to ensure regular contributions without the temptation to spend.

Moreover, Jay embraced the concept of 'geoarbitrage' – relocating to an area with a lower cost of living without sacrificing income quality. This move significantly accelerated his savings rate and allowed him to invest more into his retirement accounts.

The Mistakes That Led To Loss:

Despite his initial successes, Jay's journey wasn't without its pitfalls. Eager to boost his returns, he ventured into speculative investments without adequate research. The allure of quick profits led him to invest heavily in a single, volatile stock, diverging from his original strategy of diversification and long-term growth.

Additionally, Jay underestimated the importance of an emergency fund. When unexpected medical expenses arose, he was forced to withdraw investments at a loss, derailing his progress towards FIRE. These experiences taught Jay the value of risk management and the importance of sticking to a well-considered investment plan.

Rebuilding And Lessons Learned:

The setbacks Jay experienced were profound but not insurmountable. He returned to the core principles of the FIRE method, focusing on rebuilding his emergency fund, diversifying his investments, and maintaining his frugal lifestyle. Jay learned that discipline, patience, and adherence to a well-thought-out financial plan were crucial for long-term success.

Jay's journey to financial independence through the FIRE method is a testament to the power of perseverance, education, and strategic planning. While his path was fraught with challenges, the lessons he learned proved invaluable. For those inspired by Jay's story, the keys to success in practicing the FIRE method lie in living below one's means, investing wisely, and maintaining financial discipline, even when faced with adversity. Jay's experience serves as a reminder that while the road to financial independence may not always be smooth, with determination and the right strategies, achieving the dream of early retirement is within reach.

Chapter Summary

This chapter introduced options trading, a sophisticated investment technique that involves contracts giving the buyer the right to buy or sell an asset at a set price before a certain date. It's explained through the lens of call and put options, demonstrating their utility in speculation and risk management. The narrative showcases how investors like Sarah and Jennifer utilize options to hedge against market volatility, thus safeguarding their investments while capitalizing on market movements. The section emphasizes the importance of understanding market dynamics and the specifics of options contracts for successful trading.
The segment transitions to real estate investing,

presenting it as a method to generate income through property ownership and rental. It discusses the fundamentals of purchasing, owning, and managing property, highlighting the benefits such as rental income, property appreciation, and tax advantages. Real estate investment's potential for generating steady income and capital growth is underlined, alongside the importance of considering associated risks like market fluctuation and property maintenance.

The final section of the chapter delves into retirement planning, offering strategies to secure a financially stable future. It outlines various retirement accounts, including 401(k)s, IRAs, and pension plans, explaining their benefits and how they contribute to a comprehensive retirement strategy. The discussion extends to the FIRE method, advocating for aggressive saving and investing to achieve early financial independence. It stresses the importance of early planning, consistent saving, wise investing, and preparing for healthcare costs, aiming to provide a roadmap for a comfortable retirement.

The chapter encapsulates a holistic view of advanced investment strategies, guiding the reader from the complexities of options trading to the stability of real estate investment and the foresight required in retirement planning. It aims to equip investors with the knowledge to diversify their portfolios, manage risks, and plan for a secure financial future.

TAX-EFFICIENT INVESTING

Tax efficiency is crucial for maximizing investment returns. This chapter outlines strategies for tax-advantaged investing, starting with an overview of tax-advantaged accounts like IRAs and 401(k)s. It then explains the impact of capital gains and losses on an investor's tax liabilities and provides strategies for minimizing these liabilities. The chapter concludes with a discussion on tax-efficient asset location, offering guidance on how to allocate investments across taxable and tax-advantaged accounts to optimize tax efficiency.

Tax-Advantaged Accounts: Maximizing Benefits for Retirement Savings

Tax-advantaged investing is a strategic approach to maximizing your investments' growth by minimizing the taxes you owe. This method primarily utilizes accounts designed with tax benefits to encourage saving for retirement, education, and other long-term goals. Understanding and leveraging these accounts can significantly impact your financial future by allowing more of your money to grow through the power of compounding interest. Here's an overview of some key tax-advantaged accounts and strategies to make the most of them.

Individual Retirement Accounts (IRAs):
    Traditional IRA: Contributions may be tax-deductible depending on your income, tax filing status, and whether you're covered by a workplace retirement plan. Taxes on

earnings are deferred until withdrawals, which are taxed as ordinary income.

Roth IRA: Contributions are made with after-tax dollars, meaning they are not tax-deductible. However, both the contributions and earnings can be withdrawn tax-free in retirement, as long as certain conditions are met.

401(k)s and 403(b)s:

These are employer-sponsored retirement plans that allow employees to save and invest a portion of their paycheck before taxes are taken out. Taxes on these contributions and their earnings are deferred until the money is withdrawn in retirement. Some employers may offer a Roth option for these plans, where contributions are made with after-tax dollars, but withdrawals are tax-free in retirement.

529 Plans:

These are tax-advantaged savings plans designed to encourage saving for future education costs. Contributions grow tax-free, and withdrawals are tax-free when used for qualified education expenses.

Health Savings Accounts (HSAs):

HSAs are available to those enrolled in high-deductible health plans (HDHPs). Contributions are tax-deductible, earnings grow tax-free, and withdrawals are tax-free when used for qualified medical expenses. After reaching a certain age, funds can also be used for non-medical expenses without penalty, though they may be taxed as income.

Good retirement planners understand the importance of maximizing contributions to their tax-advantaged accounts, such as 401(k)s, IRAs (Individual Retirement Accounts), and HSAs (Health Savings Accounts), up to the maximum limits set by the IRS. This strategy is essential for several reasons:

Tax-advantaged accounts offer various tax benefits. For instance, contributions to traditional IRAs and 401(k)s may reduce your taxable income, lowering your tax bill in the contribution year. Contributions to Roth accounts are made with after-tax dollars but allow for tax-free growth and withdrawals, which can be highly beneficial in retirement.

77

Compound growth means that the earnings on your investments generate their own earnings over time. This can lead to exponential growth of your retirement funds. The more you contribute, the larger your initial base, and the greater the potential for compound growth. Even small additional contributions can significantly impact your total savings over many years.

Many employers offer a match on 401(k) contributions up to a certain percentage of your salary. By contributing enough to get the full match, you're essentially receiving free money, which also benefits from compound growth. Not taking full advantage of this is like leaving money on the table.

Regular contributions to your retirement accounts, such as through payroll deductions for a 401(k), mean that you buy more shares of investments when prices are low and fewer when prices are high. Over time, this can lower the average cost of your investments and can lead to higher long-term returns.

By consistently contributing to retirement accounts, you're practicing financial discipline, which is crucial for long-term wealth accumulation. It ensures that you're saving for your future self, reducing the temptation to spend all your income today.

The IRS sets annual contribution limits for different types of accounts. By contributing the maximum amount allowed, you're not only saving more for retirement but also taking full advantage of the tax benefits provided by these accounts. For those over 50, catch-up contributions are allowed, meaning you can contribute extra amounts to your retirement accounts, further enhancing your savings potential.

Over time, the effects of maximizing contributions, combined with compound growth, can be profound. For example, if you contribute $6,000 annually to an IRA starting at age 25, and it grows at an average annual rate of 7%, by age 65, you would have over $1.2 million. If you start the same contributions at age 35, you will have about $566,000 by age 65. This example illustrates the power of compound growth and why contributing as much as possible as early as possible can make a significant difference in your retirement savings.

Smart retirement planning involves making the highest possible contributions to tax-advantaged accounts within IRS limits, starting as early as possible, and continuing regularly. This strategy leverages tax benefits, compound growth, employer matches, and financial discipline to build a substantial retirement fund over time.

Understanding the specifics of each account type allows you to make more informed decisions about where to allocate your resources. For example, if you expect your tax rate to be higher in retirement than it is now, you might prioritize contributions to Roth accounts to benefit from tax-free withdrawals later. Alternatively, if you expect a lower tax rate in retirement, you might prefer to reduce your current taxable income through contributions to traditional accounts.

Moreover, knowing the rules helps in planning the timing and number of withdrawals to minimize taxes due while maintaining compliance with any required minimum distributions. This strategic approach to managing contributions and withdrawals across different account types can significantly reduce your tax liability over the years, enhancing the overall efficiency of your investment strategy.

A deep understanding of the distinct rules that apply to each type of tax-advantaged account can guide you in making choices that align with your financial situation and goals, ultimately leading to a more secure and tax-efficient retirement.

Converting funds from a traditional IRA or 401(k) to a Roth account is a strategic financial move known as a Roth conversion. This process involves transferring some or all the funds from your traditional, pre-tax retirement account into a Roth account, which is funded with after-tax dollars. The critical aspect of this strategy is the timing, particularly regarding your current tax status.

When you convert funds from a traditional retirement account to a Roth account, the amount transferred is added to your taxable income for that year. This means you must pay income taxes on the conversion as if the transferred amount were regular income. However, this can be a strategic advantage in years when your income is lower than usual—such as during a gap year between jobs, in early retirement before pension or Social Security benefits begin, or during any other period when your taxable income drops. In these situations, you are likely in a lower tax bracket than you were during your working years or potentially will be in the future.

The advantage of converting during these lower-income years is that you'll pay taxes on the converted amount at a lower rate than you would if you were in a higher tax bracket. While the upfront tax cost can be significant, the long-term benefits can outweigh this initial outlay. Once the funds are in the Roth account, all future growth is tax-free, as are withdrawals, provided they are qualified distributions. This means you won't owe taxes on those funds when you take them out during retirement, potentially saving you money if you would have been in a higher tax bracket at that time.

Furthermore, Roth accounts do not require minimum distributions during the lifetime of the original account holder, allowing the investments to continue growing tax-free for as long as you choose. This can provide more flexibility in managing your retirement funds and estate planning.

However, it's important to carefully consider the timing and amount of a Roth conversion. Converting a large amount in a single year could bump you into a higher tax bracket, increasing the tax impact. Therefore, some people opt to convert smaller amounts over several years to manage their tax bracket more effectively. Additionally, it's wise to consult with a financial advisor or tax professional to understand the implications fully and ensure that the strategy aligns with your overall financial plan.

In summary, a Roth conversion can be a powerful tool in retirement planning, especially when timed correctly to take advantage of lower-income years. By paying taxes at a lower rate now, you can enjoy tax-free growth and withdrawals later, providing significant financial benefits in your retirement years.

Capital Gains and Losses: Strategies for Minimizing Tax Liabilities

The strategy of using Roth accounts, such as Roth IRAs and Roth 401(k)s, for tax-free growth hinges on the accounts' unique tax treatment and can be particularly beneficial under certain circumstances.

Unlike traditional retirement accounts, where contributions may be tax-deductible and reduce your taxable income for the year they are made, contributions to Roth accounts are made with after-tax dollars. This means that you pay taxes on the money before it goes into the account, but this initial tax payment facilitates two major benefits later:

Once your money is in a Roth account, it grows tax-free. The investments within the account, whether they're stocks, bonds, or other assets, can appreciate and generate earnings. Unlike taxable accounts, you won't owe capital gains taxes or taxes on dividends each year they're earned within a Roth account.

In retirement, you can withdraw your contributions and earnings from a Roth account completely tax-free, provided you meet certain conditions (for a Roth IRA, this means you're at least 59½ years old and have held the account for at least five years). This contrasts with traditional retirement accounts, from which withdrawals are taxed as ordinary income.

Using Roth accounts for tax-free growth can be especially advantageous if you expect to be in a higher tax bracket in retirement compared to your current tax bracket. This situation might arise if you anticipate substantial income from other sources in retirement, or if tax rates increase in the future.

Furthermore, Roth accounts offer additional flexibility:

Unlike traditional IRAs and 401(k)s, Roth IRAs do not require you to start taking distributions at a certain age, allowing your investments to continue growing tax-free for your entire lifetime if you wish. This can also be a significant advantage for estate planning, as it allows you to leave tax-free assets to your heirs.

With Roth IRAs, you can withdraw your contributions (but not the earnings on those contributions) at any time, without penalty. This can provide some liquidity and financial flexibility before retirement, though it's best to let these investments grow until retirement.

Because of these benefits, contributing to Roth accounts can be a powerful strategy in your retirement planning arsenal, particularly if you aim for tax-free income in retirement or expect higher taxes in the future. However, it's important to balance the benefits of Roth contributions with your current and future financial situation, including your current tax bracket, expected future income, and the potential for legislative changes to tax laws.

Having both traditional (pre-tax) and Roth (after-tax) retirement accounts is a strategy known as tax diversification. This approach allows you to spread your investment dollars across several types of accounts with distinct tax treatments, providing several advantages, especially when it comes to managing taxes in retirement.

By having both types of accounts, you give yourself more flexibility in managing your tax situation in retirement.

Tax-Efficient Asset Location: Optimizing Portfolio Allocation for Tax Efficiency

Within tax-advantaged accounts, choosing investments that are tax-efficient plays a critical role in maximizing your financial growth. Tax-efficient investments, like index funds and ETFs (Exchange-Traded Funds), are particularly well-suited for these accounts due to their nature and structure.

Index funds and ETFs are considered tax-efficient for several reasons. Primarily, they are designed to replicate the performance of a specific index, such as the S&P 500, by holding the same stocks in the same proportions. This passive management strategy results in fewer transactions compared to actively managed funds, which frequently buy and sell holdings to try to outperform the market. Fewer transactions mean fewer taxable events, such as capital gains distributions, which can trigger a tax liability.

In a tax-advantaged account, the impact of taxes on investment returns is deferred (in the case of traditional IRAs or 401(k)s) or eliminated (in the case of Roth accounts). However, choosing tax-efficient investments like index funds and ETFs can still be beneficial. In traditional accounts, lower taxable events mean more of your money stays invested and continues to grow until you make withdrawals. In Roth accounts, while you're not taxed on withdrawals, choosing tax-efficient investments allows your money to grow more efficiently over time.

Moreover, index funds and ETFs typically have lower expense ratios than actively managed funds. Lower costs mean more of your money remains invested and compounds over time, which can significantly increase your savings in the long run.

By investing in tax-efficient funds within your tax-advantaged accounts, you're not only reducing your tax burden but also improving the overall efficiency of your investments. This approach allows your savings to grow more effectively, helping you build a larger nest egg for retirement or other financial goals.

Traditional IRAs and 401(k)s are types of retirement accounts where you can save and invest money before taxes are taken out. This means you don't pay taxes on the money when you put it in, but you will pay taxes when you take it out. There's a rule that when you reach a certain age, which is currently 72, you must start taking money out of these accounts every year. These mandatory withdrawals are called Required Minimum Distributions, or RMDs.

The amount you have to withdraw each year is based on the total balance in your accounts and your life expectancy. The idea is that you will withdraw and use this money during your retirement years, and as you do, you will pay income taxes on it.

Here's the important part: because you must withdraw this money and it counts as income, it can affect your taxes. If you have to take out a large amount, it could push you into a higher tax bracket, which means you could end up paying more taxes.

To avoid this, you can plan ahead. One strategy is to start withdrawing money from these accounts earlier than required, in smaller amounts. This can spread out the tax impact over more years. Or you might decide to convert some of your traditional IRA or 401(k) funds into a Roth IRA, where withdrawals are tax-free in retirement. However, you'll have to pay taxes on the money when you convert it, so this strategy requires careful planning.

The key is to plan your withdrawals from traditional IRAs and 401(k)s in a way that keeps your taxes as low as possible. By thinking ahead and understanding how these withdrawals can affect your tax situation, you can manage your retirement funds more effectively and potentially save money on taxes. This approach requires careful planning and, often, consultation with a financial advisor to align with your overall financial goals and retirement planning.

Chapter Summary

This chapter emphasizes the importance of tax efficiency in maximizing investment returns. It begins with an exploration of tax-advantaged accounts, highlighting their benefits in retirement savings, and how they can significantly enhance investment growth through compounding interest. The chapter discusses several types of tax-advantaged accounts, including traditional and Roth IRAs, 401(k)s, 529 Plans, and HSAs, outlining their respective tax treatments and advantages for long-term goals.

It then shifts to the impact of capital gains and losses on an investor's tax liabilities, providing strategies to minimize these liabilities. It underlines the significance of understanding how investments are taxed and offers methods to manage and reduce tax burdens associated with capital gains.

Further, the chapter delves into the concept of tax-efficient asset location, guiding readers on allocating investments between taxable and tax-advantaged accounts to optimize tax efficiency. It recommends investing in tax-efficient funds, such as index funds and ETFs, within these accounts to reduce taxable events and enhance investment growth without the drag of taxes.

Lastly, the discussion addresses the necessity of planning for Required Minimum Distributions (RMDs) from traditional IRAs and 401(k)s, which can significantly affect one's tax situation in retirement. By strategically planning withdrawals and considering conversions to Roth accounts, investors can manage their tax brackets and reduce taxes owed.

Overall, the chapter offers a comprehensive guide on using tax-advantaged investing to build a substantial retirement fund while minimizing tax liabilities, leading to a more secure and tax-efficient retirement.

MONITORING AND ADJUSTING YOUR PORTFOLIO

Maintaining and adjusting an investment portfolio is a critical practice for anyone aiming for long-term financial success. As market dynamics shift and personal circumstances evolve, a once-optimized portfolio can deviate from its intended asset allocation, potentially exposing investors to unwanted risks or missed opportunities. This chapter delves into the essential practices of rebalancing, performance evaluation, and strategic adjustment to ensure your investment portfolio remains aligned with your financial goals and risk tolerance.

Rebalancing: Maintaining Optimal Asset Allocation Over Time

Rebalancing your portfolio is a key strategy used to keep your investments aligned with your financial goals and risk tolerance. Over time, due to varying performance of different assets in your portfolio, the actual distribution of your assets can stray from your initial plan. For example, if stocks have been doing particularly well, they might become a larger portion of your portfolio than you initially decided. This can make your investments riskier than you intended.

To correct the imbalance in your portfolio, you would sell some of your stocks that have increased in value (thus "over-performing") and use the proceeds to buy more of the assets that have not done as well (the "under-performing" ones). By doing this, you bring your portfolio back to the original asset mix you had set based on your risk tolerance and investment goals.

This process is important for a couple of reasons. First, it helps maintain the level of risk you're comfortable with. If your portfolio becomes too heavy in stocks, it might expose you to more risk than you want. Second, rebalancing encourages you to follow the principle of "buying low and selling high." By selling assets that have increased in value and buying assets that are currently undervalued, you're potentially setting yourself up for better returns.

Rebalancing is a disciplined way to keep your investment strategy on track and ensure that your portfolio continues to meet your long-term financial goals and risk preferences.

Performance Evaluation: Tracking Progress Towards Financial Goals

Understanding how to measure your portfolio's performance in relation to your financial goals is a critical component of successful investing. It's not just about looking at how your investments have done compared to a market index or benchmark, although that's part of it. Truly evaluating performance means examining whether your investment strategy is guiding you towards your long-term objectives effectively.

When you assess your portfolio's performance, you're looking at several crucial factors. First, consider the ROI, or return on investment. This tells you how much your investments have grown or shrunk over a certain period. But this number doesn't mean much without context. You need to weigh it against the level of risk you've taken on. Higher returns often come with higher risks, so if your investments are doing better than expected, make sure it's not because you're unknowingly taking on too much risk.

Also, factor in the cost of your investments. Fees and expenses can eat into your returns significantly over time, so it's essential to know how much you're paying and whether you're getting good value.

Beyond these financial metrics, performance evaluation is also about reflecting on changes in your personal life. Life events like marriage, the birth of a child, or getting closer to retirement can significantly impact your financial goals and how much risk you're comfortable taking. For example, as you approach retirement, you might want to shift towards a more conservative investment approach to protect your savings. Conversely, if you're far from retirement and have just started a family, you might decide to take on more risk to grow your savings over the long term.

Accurately measuring your portfolio's performance involves a comprehensive approach that goes beyond simple return rates. It requires assessing how well your investments align with your evolving financial goals, risk tolerance, and life circumstances, ensuring that your strategy remains appropriate as your life and the markets change.

Adjusting Strategies: Adapting to Changing Market Conditions and Life Events

An effective investment strategy should be adaptable, changing as your life circumstances and market conditions change. It's not something you can set once and forget about. As you move through separate phases of your life, your financial needs, goals, and risk tolerance are likely to change. For instance, as you get closer to retirement, you might want to reduce your risk by shifting more of your investments into bonds or other more conservative assets. This helps protect your savings from major market downturns when you have less time to recover from losses.

On the other hand, if you're early in your career and have many years until retirement, you might decide to increase your investment in stocks or other higher-risk assets. This can offer higher returns over the long term, helping to build your wealth. Similarly, if you receive a significant raise or come into a financial windfall, you might choose to invest more aggressively, taking advantage of your improved ability to absorb risk.

Your investment strategy should also respond to the broader economic and financial environment. Changes in tax laws can affect the efficiency of different investment vehicles, potentially altering which options are most beneficial for you. Inflation rates can erode the purchasing power of your savings, making it important to choose investments that can outpace inflation. Global events, such as economic downturns or political instability, can impact markets and influence your investment decisions.

To manage these dynamics effectively, regular review and adjustment of your investment portfolio are essential. This doesn't mean reacting to every market fluctuation—doing so can lead to poor decision-making. Instead, it means periodically reviewing your portfolio to ensure it aligns with your current financial goals, risk tolerance, and the economic landscape. By staying informed and making thoughtful, well-informed adjustments, you can keep your investment strategy aligned with your long-term objectives, helping to ensure that your portfolio remains effective regardless of how your personal circumstances, or the world around you, changes.

Maintaining and adjusting your investment portfolio is an ongoing process that plays a vital role in achieving financial success. By regularly rebalancing, evaluating performance, and adjusting strategies as necessary, you can ensure that your investment efforts are consistently aligned with your changing financial needs and market conditions. This dynamic approach to investment management will help you stay on course towards achieving your long-term financial goals while managing risk effectively.

Chapter Summary

This chapter emphasizes the importance of regular maintenance and adjustment of investment portfolios for long-term financial success. It outlines the necessity of rebalancing to keep investments aligned with financial goals and risk tolerance. This involves selling over-performing assets and buying underperforming ones to maintain the original asset allocation, which helps control risk levels and encourages the discipline of buying low and selling high.

It also highlights the significance of evaluating portfolio performance beyond just comparing returns against benchmarks. Effective evaluation considers return on investment, risk levels, costs, and personal life changes like marriage or approaching retirement, ensuring that investment strategies stay relevant to evolving goals and circumstances.

Additionally, the chapter advises on adjusting investment strategies in response to life events, market conditions, and economic changes, such as tax law revisions or inflation, to protect savings or capitalize on growth opportunities. Regular portfolio reviews and informed adjustments are recommended to keep investment strategies aligned with personal financial objectives, ensuring that portfolios remain effective over time regardless of external changes. This proactive approach to investment management is key to navigating market fluctuations and achieving long-term financial goals while managing risk.

CONCLUSION

In this closing chapter, we synthesize the key concepts and strategies detailed throughout the book, underscoring the imperative role of financial literacy in personal and economic empowerment. We delve into the significance of proactive financial planning and the necessity of employing smart money management techniques. The goal is to inspire you, dear reader, to apply these principles diligently to navigate the complexities of personal finance successfully.

Recap of Key Concepts and Strategies

The book explored various critical financial themes: budgeting, saving, investing, debt management, and planning. Each topic is woven with the thread of financial literacy, demonstrating how understanding your finances is the first step toward control and growth. We've highlighted the need for a solid budget, the power of an emergency fund, the wisdom in avoiding unnecessary debt, and the long-term benefits of consistent investing.

Financial literacy is not just about numbers; it's about making informed choices that lead to a secure and fulfilling life. We've discussed how understanding financial principles can safeguard against common pitfalls and open doors to new opportunities. It's the foundation upon which sound financial decisions are built.

Encouragement for Acting and Making Smart Money Moves

Waiting for the 'right moment' to start planning is one of the biggest mistakes one can make. Take immediate action, regardless of your current financial status. We've shown how proactive measures, like setting financial goals, preparing for emergencies, and regularly reviewing financial plans, can significantly impact your financial well-being.

We've provided strategies and tools for managing your money effectively. From creating a budget that works for you to understanding the power of compounding interest in investments, these techniques are designed to help you maximize your financial resources.

Resources for Further Learning and Support

To further your journey beyond these pages, we offer a comprehensive list of resources:

- Websites like Investopedia, NerdWallet, and The Financial Diet offer a wealth of information on various financial topics.
- Consider classic books like "The Richest Man in Babylon" by George S. Clason, or "Rich Dad Poor Dad" by Robert Kiyosaki for foundational financial wisdom.
- Look for local financial planning workshops or online webinars hosted by financial experts.
- Utilize budgeting apps and investment platforms like Mint or Personal Capital to manage your finances efficiently.

Our core message is simple yet profound: take charge of your financial destiny. By applying the principles of smart monetary management, you are not merely surviving; you are thriving. We encourage you to not only apply what you have learned but also to remain curious and continue your financial education.

As you turn the final page of this book, view it not as the end, but as the beginning of your empowered financial journey. Let the principles and strategies you've learned be the tools that guide you toward a more secure and prosperous future. Remember, the path to financial success is a lifelong journey of learning and growth. Financial mastery is within your grasp. By embracing the principles discussed throughout this book, you can build a robust financial future. Take the first step today, and never stop learning, planning, and growing. *Your financial future is in your hands.*

ABOUT THE AUTHOR

Russell N. Hatcher completed his education at the University of Florida College of Pharmacy. He embarked on a professional journey that took him through various facets of finance, including investment banking, financial planning, and wealth management. His diverse experience has equipped him with a unique perspective on the financial challenges and opportunities facing Americans today.

In addition to his professional endeavors, Russell is an avid writer and communicator. He has been a contributor to several magazines and blogs, where he simplifies complex concepts for the everyday reader. His approachable style and practical advice have earned him a loyal following among those looking to navigate the often-intimidating world of complex themes and ideas.

"Smart Money Moves: A Practical Guide to Personal Finance and Investing" is Russell's debut book about finance, born out of his desire to empower individuals to take control of their financial future. Through this book, he aims to share his wealth of knowledge and research, providing readers with the tools they need to make informed financial decisions and achieve their personal and financial goals.

When he's not writing, Russell enjoys spending time with his family, exploring the great outdoors, and continuing his own education. He believes that learning is a lifelong journey and is always looking for new ways to expand his knowledge and skills. Russell resides with his family in Florida.

BIBLIOGRAPHY

'I Will Teach You to Be Rich' Founder Ramit Sethi Shares His Secrets to Success. (n.d.). Retrieved 2 25, 2024, from http://fortune.com/2017/01/05/ramit-sethi-i-will-teach-you-to-be-rich/

Benjamin Graham, J. Z. (2003). *The Intelligent Investor: The Definitive Book on Value Investing.* Retrieved 2 25, 2024, from https://books.google.com/books?id=klYquu4H1wAC&pg=PA242#v=onepage&q&f=false

Financial Concepts: Random Walk Theory. (n.d.). Retrieved 2 25, 2024, from Investopedia: http://www.investopedia.com/university/concepts/concepts5.asp

Larimore, T., & Lindauer, M. (Eds.). (n.d.). *The Bogleheads' Guide to Retirement Planning.* Wiley. Retrieved 2 25, 2024

Moriarty, R. (2016). *Nobody Knows Anything: Investing Basics.*

Strakal, D. (2005). Rich Dad, Poor Dad: What the Rich Teach Their Kids about Money That the Poor and Middle Class Do Not. *The Career Planning and Adult Development Journal, 21*(3), 127. Retrieved 2 25, 2024, from https://questia.com/library/journal/1p3-1266718981/rich-dad-poor-dad-what-the-rich-teach-their-kids